God's
Vitamin "C"
for the
Christmas
Spirit™

Compiled by **Kathy Collard Miller** *and* **D. Larry Miller**

STARBURST PUBLISHERS

P.O. Box 4123, Lancaster, Pennsylvania 17604

To schedule Author appearances write:Author Appearances, Starburst Promotions, P.O. Box 4123, Lancaster, Pennsylvania 17604 or call (717) 293-0939.

Credits:
Cover by David Marty Design
Page design and illustrations by Bill Dussinger

Unless otherwise noted, or paraphrased by the author, all Scripture quotations are from the King James Version of The Holy Bible.

We, the Publisher and Authors, declare that to the best of our knowledge all material (quoted or not) contained herein is accurate, and we shall not be held liable for the same.

First Printing, September 1996
ISBN: 0-914984-85-3
Library of Congress Catalog Number 96-068840
Printed in the United States of America

The Christmas Story

In those days Caesar Augustus issued a decree that a census should be taken of the entire Roman world. (This was the first census that took place while Quirinius was governor of Syria.) And everyone went to his own town to register.

So Joseph also went up from the town of Nazareth in Galilee to Judea, to Bethlehem the town of David, because he belonged to the house and line of David. He went there to register with Mary, who was pledged to be married to him and was expecting a child. While they were there, the time came for the baby to be born, and she gave birth to her firstborn, a son. She wrapped him in cloths and placed him in a manger, because there was no room for them in the inn.

And there were shepherds living out in the fields nearby, keeping watch over their flocks at night. An angel of the Lord appeared to them, and the glory of the Lord shone around them, and they were terrified. But the angel said to them "Do not be afraid. I bring you good news of great joy that will be for all the people. Today in the town of David a Savior has been born to you; he is Christ the Lord. This will be a sign

to you: You will find a baby wrapped in cloths and lying in a manger."

Suddenly a great company of the heavenly host appeared with the angel, praising God and saying, "Glory to God in the highest, and on earth peace to men on whom his favor rests."

When the angels had left them and gone into heaven, the shepherds said to one another, "Let's go to Bethlehem and see this thing that has happened, which the Lord has told us about."

So they hurried off and found Mary and Joseph, and the baby, who was lying in the manger. When they had seen him, they spread the word concerning what had been told them about this child, and all who heard it were amazed at what the shepherds said to them. But Mary treasured up all these things and pondered them in her heart. The shepherds returned, glorifying and praising God for all the things they had heard and seen, which were just as they had been told.

Luke 2:1-20 NIV

4

The Jesus Stocking

Because our oldest child's birthday is six days before Christmas, she has often received Christmas gifts in lieu of birthday gifts. When she was three, a friend gave her a huge Christmas stocking for her birthday.

Since I had already handmade a Christmas stocking for each of us that were the same size, we decided to give the big Christmas stocking to Jesus. Carefully we wrote His name across the large white fold at the top of the stocking for all to see.

Every year this stocking is traditionally hung in a prominent place near the Christmas tree. In it we each place a personal gift to Jesus in the form of a letter (when the children were small, they would draw a special picture as their gift), sharing with Him individual hopes, dreams, prayer requests and things for which to be thankful. This letter (or drawing) is to remain private—only between the giver and the Lord. It is dated and signed and placed in the person's individual envelope with all the "stocking gifts" from previous years and put into the stocking.

Each year we pull out our individual envelopes and read through

the previously-written communications. We are always fascinated as we see our personal growth as well as what was important to us in the past. For the girls, who began this process early in life, it has given them a measuring point of their own progress from drawing pictures to writing letters, as well as a starting place for their own personal relationship with the Lord.

The writing of the annual letter has become a Christmas Eve tradition, which sometimes becomes more difficult to hold to as the children get older and schedules become more complicated. It has now become a very personal process. When the girls begin their own homes, we will give them a "Jesus stocking" of their own, along with their personal envelope, should they choose to carry on the tradition.

This year we added a new step to our Christmas tradition of the Jesus Stocking—the Christmas Nail. Purchased at a local Christian bookstore, the Christmas Nail is the last gift to be opened under the tree. Its purpose is to help us refocus on the meaning of Christmas after all the gifts have been opened and the stress of shopping and Christmas programs has fallen to the wayside. The Christmas Nail will remain in a prominent place in our living area throughout the year and be rewrapped at Christmas to again remind us of the ever-giving love and sacrifice of the Lord Jesus on our behalf.

—Christi Anne Sheppeard

6

And To All A Good Night

After Christmas many years ago, three elementary school-aged boys played with their new toys until they were tired of them— three days or so.

Their mother brought an empty cardboard box into the dining room, sat the boys down, and told them of underprivileged boys at a local orphanage who each got a piece of fruit, a candy bar, a comb, and a cheap toy in a standard package.

"Merry Christmas," one of the brothers said with sarcasm.

Their mother nodded, brows arched. "How about we give some of those guys a Christmas they won't forget?"

They sat silent. She continued.

"Let's fill this box with toys that will make Christmas special. We'll do what Jesus would do."

One of the brothers had an idea. "With all my new stuff, I don't need all my old stuff!"

He ran to get armloads full of dingy, dilapidated toys, but when he returned, his mother's look stopped him. "Is that what Jesus would do?"

He pursed his lips and shrugged. "You want us to give our new stuff?"

7

"It's just a suggestion."

"All of it?"

"I didn't have in mind all of it. Just whatever toys you think."

"I'll give this car," one said, placing it in the box.

"If you don't want it," another said. "I'll take it."

"I'm not givin' it to you; I'm givin' it to the orphans."

"I'm done with this bow and arrow set," another said.

"I'll take that," another chimed in.

"I'll trade you these pens for that model."

"No deals but I'll take the pens and the cap gun."

The boys hardly noticed their mother leave the room. The box sat there, empty and glaring. The boys idly slipped away and played on the floor. But there was none of the usual laughing, arguing, roughhousing. Each played with his favorite toys with renewed vigor.

One by one the boys visited the kitchen. It was a small house and that was the only place their mother could be.

Each found her sitting at the table, her coat and hat and gloves on. Her face had that fighting tears look. No words were exchanged.

The boys got the picture. She wasn't going to browbeat her sons into

8

filling that box. No guilt trips, no pressure. It had been a suggestion. Each returned to play quietly, as if in farewell to certain toys and to selfishness.

A few minutes later, their mother came for the box. The eldest had carefully and resolutely placed almost all his new toys in it. The others selected more carefully but chose the best for the box. Their mother took the box to the car without a word, an expression, or a gesture. She never reported on the reception of the orphans, and she was never asked.

Several years of childhood remained, but childishness had been dealt a blow.

—Jerry B. Jenkins

9

Priceless Gift

During years of giving and receiving Christmas gifts, I have received four that have immeasurable worth to me.

My first Christmas with my husband, Steve, was filled with warmth and happiness. Though money was scarce, Steve gave me a small, white vase with three roses. The simple beauty of the roses and the sincere expression on Steve's face told me those roses represented so much that was true and lovely.

With help from a camera, the image of those roses remains a sweet memory for me to cherish in my heart.

The second unforgettable gift was given to me by our son, Nathan. Christmas came in the middle of our second year of home-schooling. Nathan gave me a lidded basket with dried flowers glued on top. Inside the basket was a card inscribed, "Thank you, Mom, for teaching me to read."

Now, years later, when I see Nathan's Bible lying beside his bed where he reads it each night, I remember that basket and note of thanks.

The third special gift came from my mother. At Christmastime

our large family draws names for gift-giving, and my mom had drawn my name.

In October of that year Mom had been diagnosed with cancer. And in mid-November my brother's 12-year-old daughter, Aimee, lost her battle with cystic fibrosis.

Mom's gift to me changed a Christmas that I didn't want to remember into one that I will never forget. Mom made an audio-cassette tape about her childhood and told many stories that I had never heard before. During that time of pain, disease, grief and dying, Mother shared her life with me.

That cassette tape, a treasure beyond all measure, is safely pro-tected inside a drawer.

Our daughter, Heidi, gave me the fourth special gift. When she was about four years old, Heidi jumped up and down with excite-ment as I opened a tiny package. Inside a ball of Christmas wrap and tape was a plastic bag which held a tiny nativity scene with Mary, Joseph and the Baby Jesus.

"Mommy, Jesus glows in the dark," Heidi kept saying. She was right. Her little glow-in-the-dark nativity scene did shine through the darkness; it has continued to be a reminder of God's greatest Gift.

11

I know that the Savior is with me even when times are dark and gloomy. He is the Light to my path. Heidi's gift reminds me of that truth.

Faded roses, a yellowed card inside a small basket, an audiocassette with words from my mother, a plastic nativity scene—treasures I wouldn't trade for millions of dollars. Priceless gifts have nothing to do with monetary value. Jesus, born in a musty, smelly stable, proved that long ago.

—Annie Chapman

Christmas Card Activities

Christmas Card Devotions

Cards can be used as a meaningful part of family devotions during the Advent season.

• Each day (or on selected days) use the cards received on that particular day, or have someone pull a specific number of cards from a basket used for this purpose.

• During family devotions, or after singing or Bible study, read the cards aloud.

• Have prayer for the families who sent the cards.

• Hang the cards up for display on the mantel, around a doorway or archway, on the back of a door, or on the Christmas tree.

Christmas Card Prayer Link

Use Christmas cards as a link to real people and their needs through the Christmas season and the month of January.

• Choose one Christmas card each day from those received. Read the whole card aloud and pass it around the family circle. (Do this at a

regular time like bedtime or after supper each night or at breakfast time.)

• Have special prayer together for each person in the family that sent the card.

• Send a postcard to that family to tell them about your Christmas card prayers and that their card was the one chosen on this day. They will appreciate knowing that your family prayed today for their family.

After Christmas Cards

• As Christmas cards come, place them in an attractive container. After Christmas is over and the household is more settled, place the container near the dinner table.

• After dinner, pass the container and let each member of the family choose one card.

• Take turns reading the cards and enjoying their beauty.

• Discuss the family or person who sent the card. Are there any specific problems or needs?

• Close your dinner hour by praying for the families or persons who sent the cards.

—Shirley Dobson and Gloria Gaither

14

Giving in Secret

One family has an interesting tradition of giving. Each Christmas they look around to see whom they might give to that year. Once they have selected the person, they set aside a portion of their family Christmas resources to make an anonymous contribution to that needy person's holiday cheer.

One year they noticed an older woman in town who lived on a fixed income. They watched her to see what she might need, and decided on a beautiful, warm sweater. Their joy was extended as they saw her wear that sweater day in and day out during the long, cold winter.

Another year they spotted a little girl from a family in their church and realized that they had never seen her in a dress. They picked out a lovely dress with shoes to match, which they wrapped and sent anonymously. Every Sunday thereafter that little girl wore that pretty dress and shoes to church.

The parents of this generous family enjoy this tradition a great deal, but it has become their boys' favorite part of the Christmas season.

—Cheri Fuller

15

Silent Night

Not a sound would come forth from the pipe organ in the church. Not even a single note! In despair, organist Franz Gruber rushed to tell the priest, Father Joseph Mohr. "Mice have eaten through the bellows! There is no way to repair the organ in time for the Christmas Eve service."

The news struck Father Mohr like a thunderbolt. No music for Christmas Eve . . . in the church of St. Nicholas? That would be unthinkable! The little Bavarian village of Oberndorf lay half-buried in snow. No repairman from the outside world could possibly reach them—and it was already Christmas Eve morning!

"What can we do, what can we do?" wailed Herr Gruber, wringing his hands and pacing up and down.

For a moment Father Mohr, too, was caught by fear and anxiety. Then, suddenly calm, he said, "We will pray!"

Astonished, Franz Gruber stopped pacing. How simple Father Mohr made it all sound! "Why, of course!" he agreed. "We will pray."

The two men embraced and soon parted as Father Joseph Mohr, wearing his warmest coat, set out upon his round of parish calls.

16

There were many calls to make; much help and comfort to be given to the sick and the poor—especially at Christmas time.

Suddenly Father Mohr received a hurried and special summons. In a humble cottage on the outskirts of the village, the woodcutter's wife had just given birth to a child. So, on through the snowdrifts the priest trudged in order to welcome and bless the new baby.

It was early evening when Father Mohr returned home, warmed by the memory of the scene he had witnessed that afternoon; the tiny face of the woodcutter's "Christmas Eve child" nestled in its mother's arms. His mind wandered back over the centuries to that first Christmas Eve. Vividly he pictured the newborn Christ Child, sleeping in His mother's arms. Longing to share this vision with his congregation, Father Mohr took up his pen. Effortlessly, words began to flow and soon, with a new poem in hand, he hurried to his friend, the organist Franz Gruber.

"Franz, dear friend, please write a tune to go with my poem; something simple that can be sung at the midnight service to the accompaniment of a guitar."

"But there is not enough time . . . " protested the organist.

"Have faith," urged Father Mohr, his eyes smiling, "God will provide the melody."

17

Slowly Franz Gruber read the poem. "Beautiful!" he exclaimed. And as he read and re-read the inspiring words, he began to hum a simple melody. Soon both men were humming, then singing: "Stille Nacht, Heilige Nacht . . . "

Silent Night! Holy Night! All is calm, all is bright!
Round yon Virgin, Mother and Child,
Holy Infant so tender and mild,
Sleep in heavenly peace, Sleep in heavenly peace.

And so it happened that on Christmas Eve in 1818, in the candle-lit church of St. Nicholas, the villagers of Oberndorf in Bavaria were the first to hear this beautiful and moving carol. And now, each year millions of people around the world join in caroling this song to express their joy and love through the words and music of:

Silent Night, Holy Night . . .
With the Angels let us sing, Alleluia to our King;
Christ the Savior is born. Christ the Savior is born.

—Mala Powers

18

A Candymaker's Witness

A candymaker in Indiana wanted to make a candy that would be a testimony of the true meaning of Christmas. So he invented the Christmas Candy Cane. The candyman incorporated several symbols for the birth, ministry, and death of Jesus Christ. He began with a stick of pure white hard candy: "white" to symbolize the Virgin Birth and the sinless nature of Jesus, and "hard" to symbolize the Solid Rock, the foundation of the Church, and firmness of the promises of God.

The candymaker made the candy in the form of a "J" to represent the precious name of Jesus, who came to earth as our Savior. It could also represent the staff of the "Good Shepherd" with which He reaches down into the ditches of the world to lift out the fallen lambs who, like all sheep, have gone astray.

Thinking that the candy was somewhat plain, the candymaker stained it with red stripes. He used small stripes to show the stripes of the scourging Jesus received by which we are "healed" from our sin. The large red stripe was for the blood shed by Christ on the cross so that we could have the promise of eternal life.

This Christmas symbol, the candy cane, can remind you of the true meaning of Christmas as you celebrate it this year.

19

Christmas Came Anyway

It was Christmas Eve during wartime. We lived 10 miles from town in a one-room rented cabin without electricity, indoor plumbing, or running water. It was not exactly my dream of our first Christmas together.

I straightened my back and shifted my bulky six-months pregnant body to reach for some red tissue paper. Through misty eyes, I wrapped my husband's only present—three handkerchiefs on which I'd embroidered his initials.

Where would I hide his gift until morning? Our cabin had no cupboards and no closets. Oh well, I thought, I guess I'll give it to him when he gets home from work. It sure doesn't feel like Christmas!

I listened for the sound of truck tires on the dirt and gravel drive. Red would be home from work soon, bringing a filled water can. Every day my husband took one empty milk can with him to fill with water on his way home from work. Every day I prayed for an apartment or little house with inside utilities.

With a sigh of relief, I heard familiar truck tires scrunch on the

20

gravel drive. Cold air blew inside as Red rolled the tall milk can with our water supply across the floor to its corner. I snuggled into his embrace and looked up at his pleased-with-himself grin.

"I bought a Christmas tree," he said. "It's in the truck. I'll be right back."

A tree? Where does he think we'll put it? My thoughts followed him out the door.

My husband marched in, triumphantly bearing a foot-and-a-half tall, lopsided pine tree. Setting it firmly on the corner of the table, he tore open a sack of candy canes and a packet of tinsel. Gloomily, I stared at the red and white candy bending those tiny branches. With a flourish, my husband draped each tip with silvery strands.

I knew Christmas was more than a beautifully decorated tree, a nice home with conveniences, and a festive dinner with pretty table settings. I knew Christmas was the celebration of Jesus' coming to live among us. However, somehow I'd hoped for more than what we had at the moment.

Red put his arms around me, drawing me close. This was a difficult time for him, too. He wanted to be a better provider.

"It is pretty—kind of funny pretty," I said.

21

Tinsel shimmered in the light of the lantern. The whole room seemed to glow. Holding hands, we stood there in wonder at that tiny, tilting tree—and we felt Christmas.

Slipping from Red's embrace, I held out the red tissue-wrapped package. "Merry Christmas, honey."

He reached inside his coat pocket. "Hope you like it." He twisted the key on the bottom of a little music box and placed it in my hands.

My fingers closed around my gift—a plain, gold-painted metal container. It had a dome-shaped top with three miniature wooden legs. No figurine danced around; no decorations adorned it. The key tickled my hand as it turned. Nodding in time to the notes I whispered the words, "I'll be loving you always, always."

As tinkling notes filled the room, my eyes filled with tears, too. Swallowing hard, I hugged my husband. "Merry Christmas, Babe," he said softly.

Nestled in his arms, I remembered the light and the song surrounding another couple thousands of years ago in a much humbler dwelling. In the glow of our lamp-lighted cabin, my heart heard an angel choir and Christmas came.

—June L. Varnum

22

The Origin of the Crèche

The crèche (literally "crib") is believed to have its origins with St. Francis of Assisi. He was concerned because the people seemed not to understand what Christ's birth was like or fully appreciate the events surrounding his birth in a barn with animals in attendance; how the shepherds on the hillside were surprised by the angels or how the Three Kings came from far away to pay homage to the Babe.

In 1223 Francis created the first known crèche—a real-life reenactment of Christ's birth—at the church in Greccio, near Assisi, Italy. At first he included a newborn baby in a manger and Mary and Joseph. In the following years he added the other participants in the nativity story. On Christmas Eve people came from nearby villages to see the scene. This popular custom quickly spread throughout Europe.

You may already count a crèche, or nativity scene, as one of your Christmas decorations. In many families the crèche consists of a small wooden stable, figures of Mary, Joseph, and the Babe in a manger, and perhaps shepherds, assorted animals, angels, and Wise Men. Often the original set has been lovingly extended by the addition of modeled or plaster-of-Paris figurines that children have made in school or at

23

church. Other items have been added: an aluminum-foil star on top of the stable, fiberglass "snow" on which to place the scene, and plastic animals from a child's farm set.

Ready-made crèches of all sizes and descriptions are sold during the Christmas season, but they may also be modeled from clay (professional modeling compound or salt-and-flour type), made by painting and firing ceramic greenware carved from soap or wood, or created by children who employ their own imaginations and materials: Barbie and Ken wrapped in scraps of cloth to resemble Mary and Joseph, Strawberry Shortcake for the Babe, a cardboard box with glued-on hay fashioned to look like a stable, with favorite stuffed animals in attendance.

If we remember St. Francis' concern that the people be able to see graphically what the first nativity was like, then we will look on our own crèche differently. While there are beautiful and expensive sets to be had, there is also a special meaning when a child's favorite dolls or play figures are used to tell the Christmas story. This reminds him that God chose ordinary people and commonplace events to attend the miraculous birth of Christ. The old and chipped plaster figurines from our own childhood, which we faithfully display year after year, under-

24

line the rich tradition and meaning of Christmas. Time spent painting greenware, carving figures, or building our own stable, provides opportunity for quiet reflection as we create with our own hands symbols that, for years to come, will remind us of God's wonderful gift.

It has been the custom among some ethnic groups to display the nativity scene with an empty manger, and then to add the Christchild on Christmas Eve. The Wise Men may be placed in a far part of the room and moved closer to the stable each day after the appearance of the Babe until they finally arrive at the stable on Epiphany, the twelfth day after Christmas. Shepherds may similarly be placed at a distance so that they can make their symbolic journey to see the child after he has been born.

—Alice Slaikeu Lawhead

The Jesus Box

We all have many traditions in our families. These traditions span throughout cultures and religions, many being passed down from generation to generation. In our family we enjoy beginning new traditions as well as practicing the old ones. Each year we try to come up with something new and interesting and integrate it with the others. There is one in particular that has been a real joy and was started years ago when my children were very young.

I wanted to emphasize the point that gifts, or how much we spend on them, were not that important. That it was "better to give than to receive" all of those things that we all want our children to learn. I also wanted them to understand that the money we give to the offering each week actually goes to Jesus! I thought that they should know how Jesus uses that money to help others or the church in one way or another. So, we decided that instead of dropping a check into the offering plate during the month of December, we would do something a little different that would involve the children as well.

We usually put up our Christmas decorations right after

26

Thanksgiving, and at that time we also set up the Manger Scene (or crèche). This particular year when we had finished setting Mary and Joseph in their assigned spots by Baby Jesus, along with the Wise Men, we took a little box, the one that our checks came in, and wrapped it with pretty Christmas paper and a little bow. We added a name tag which read: "TO JESUS, WITH LOVE FROM THE LEWIS FAMILY."

We wrapped the box so the lid could come off and on easily, then we placed it by the Manger Scene in plain view, where it remained for the month of December. I explained, "The box is here for you to give an offering whenever you feel you want to."

My husband continued, "And when you do, stop for a moment and say a little prayer for a family member, a friend, or for God to use the money for His glory . . . or whatever is on your heart."

Throughout the month of December, family members, at their own discretion, would stop to place an offering in the "Jesus Box" and say a prayer. Sometimes it would be a few cents and sometimes it would be a few dollars. The amount never matters, it's the gift of the heart that counts.

27

What a joy it is to see one of my children take the only two pennies they own and put them in the "Jesus Box," then reverently bow their head to say a prayer. Or to see my grown teenage son or husband kneeling before the Lord asking Him to bless the twenty dollars he has placed in the box that would have otherwise been spent on pizza.

On Christmas Sunday we take the "Jesus Box," our gift, to church with us. When the offering plate comes around, one of our children places the whole box in the plate. As we watch it being passed down the aisle, I can see the happiness, joy, excitement and fulfillment in my children's faces, something that would have been missed if we hadn't involved them.

It has been many years since we started the "Jesus Box," and through it we have learned commitment and obedience to God's Word about tithing. I think Christmas would not be the same without it.

—Deborah M. Lewis

28

The Christmas Feathers

It was the day after Thanksgiving and I was plenty worried. I had bought Christmas presents a few days before: dish towels for Mom, white socks for Dad, and toy cars for my brothers. After counting the money in my wallet I discovered that all I had left was forty-two cents. How had I forgotten about the stockings?

Saturday morning, after chores, we watched cartoons and waited for Mom to start the tradition. It wasn't long until she called me into the living room.

"Bring me the hammer from the kitchen tool box, please."

I took it to her. After a lot of pounding, mom got the nail in the old hole and wrapped the wire around it to string across the fireplace for hanging the stockings.

"What do you think, Morgan? Look pretty festive?" asked mom.

"Sure does, Mom." I knew what she would say next. Maybe there will be something in them before nightfall.

"Maybe there will be something in them before nightfall," she said happily.

That day, before lunch, there was something in all the stock-

ings— except Mom's. We all knew she had put the things in the socks, but she wouldn't talk. I checked with the other boys and they didn't have anything for the stockings either. By supper time there was one more thing in the stockings— except Mom's. I thought I could feel a new pocket knife in my stocking; but I couldn't be sure.

I knew Mom was feeling left out because there was nothing in her stocking and it was almost time for Christmas Cheer. While she was in the kitchen, I went upstairs to my room to think. What did I have to put in her stocking? She always says it is the thought that counts. But I didn't have many thoughts.

I looked through the drawers of my desk, but didn't find anything that would work. Paper clips or pencils didn't seem right, neither did rubber bands or a ruler. Then I saw my feather collection. I had collected thirty feathers that summer and poked the ends into a short plastic tube I had found in the park. The bird feathers were many different colors, and I had found one from a cardinal and one from a bluejay.

I snuck down the stairs and stuffed my feather collection in Mom's stocking. Landon saw me.

"What are you doing? She'll hate that," he said.

"Why?"

30

"You know she's afraid of spiders and stuff."

"Feathers aren't spiders."

"No, but they're from birds, and I don't think she likes birds much either. She wouldn't let me get that parakeet I wanted."

I was going to take the feather collection out of Mom's stocking, but she came in the room as I reached for it.

Her eyes lit up when she saw her stocking. "Something's in my stocking," she said and walked over to feel it. "Whatever can it be?"

I looked at my brother Landon, and he looked at me. There was no way I could take it out now.

Two weeks later all the decorations were up. Every decoration my brothers and I had ever made in school were on the walls, and we had decorated the Christmas tree. We had Christmas Cheer in the living room by the fireplace—so we could look at the stockings during the lighting ceremony when Dad put the star on top of the tree.

I had wrapped my presents and put them under the tree. By adding another two weeks' allowance to my money, I had enough to buy packs of gum (I like gum) to put in everyone's stocking; including my own. But I kept thinking about that feather collection. Maybe Landon was wrong. I loved it, so why wouldn't Mom?

31

On Christmas morning we lit a fire and played Christmas music while Mom plugged in the coffeepot. Then we tackled our stockings. I got a pocket knife— just like I had wanted, and disappearing ink, gum, poster paints, a new belt, two candy bars, an apple and an orange. What a haul!

"Morgan."

I looked up when Mom said my name. She was holding my feather collection and looked like she was going to cry. "She hates it!" I thought. Landon was right, it was a dumb idea.

"Morgan," she said again. "I will treasure your feather collection always. This is a gift from the heart, the most special kind. Thank you, Morgan. I'll keep it in my desk and whenever you want to see it or add to it, you may."

She smiled at me with her eyes all shiny— I will never forget that Christmas as long as I live.

—Veda Boyd Jones

The Gift of Eternity

In Ecclesiastes King Solomon wrote, "He hath set eternity in their heart." I heard a story that sums up what Solomon had in mind. An English post office clerk, whose job it was to handle letters that were inadequately addressed, was at his desk on Christmas Eve. He was brokenhearted because death had taken his little son. He was given a letter addressed in childlike writing to "Santa Claus, The North Pole." Attached to it was a note from a postman giving the address where he had picked up the letter. The clerk was startled because it was his own address. The writing was that of his daughter. And the letter said:

"We're very sad at our house this year. My little brother went to heaven last week."

"You needn't leave me anything. But if you could give Daddy something that would make him stop crying, I wish you would. I heard him say to Mommy that only eternity can cure him. Could you send him some of that?"

We all need the gift of eternity, and it can be ours now.

—Billy Graham

33

A Christmas Offering

As a child I always had the honor of carrying out our family tradition of delivering a plate of our favorite holiday cookies and candies to our next-door neighbors at Christmastime. And this Christmas, although I was now an adult all alone in a big city over a thousand miles from home, would be no different.

My baking vigil began two days before Christmas and, accompanied by Christmas carols, lasted late into the night. Piles of rich, chocolate fudge loaded with pecans began to grow on my breakfast nook. Walnut-studded divinity competed for space, along with nut logs dusted with powdered sugar, green and pink Spritz cookies pressed into Christmas trees and stars, and peanut butter cookies in the shape of camels. Icing was squeezed into split dates with almonds.

What started as a fierce determination not to cry at being alone on Christmas was turning into an adventure. Excitedly, I loaded the goodies on cheery holiday plates enveloped with red crinkly cellophane. Then I secured it all with big green bows. "Merry Christmas from your neighbor in Apartment 201," read the attached card.

My enthusiasm suddenly turned to fear. Oh, Lord, what if they are all

34

diabetic or on a diet? What if everybody went out of town for Christmas? The cookies may sit there forever. What if they're afraid to eat them? They don't know me.

Have I been presumptuous AGAIN? To think that I could possibly do anything right. I messed up again, didn't I? Overzealous. No sense at all. Oh, well, I've already spent two days baking. I might as well go through with it and make a fool of myself.

On Christmas Eve I made my journey to the various apartments. Much to my relief, no one answered their doorbell, so I left the Christmas offerings at the doors. I would double-check tomorrow to see if the packages had been rescued.

In a few days, an elderly lady next door motioned me to come into her apartment. "Thank you so much for your thoughtfulness. I am diabetic, but when my bridge group came this week I proudly brought out the array of splendid cookies and fudge you left. Everyone loved the treats!"

So she is diabetic. Well, it's the thought that counts, I mumbled to myself.

Next I received an invitation to go upstairs to visit a woman and her grown daughter. "It's a pleasure to meet you. We don't get many visitors because they feel uncomfortable with my daughter's Down Syndrome."

I didn't realize a few cookies could mean so much. I was beginning to sense God's hand in this. Thank you, Lord.

But what really struck my heart was something I heard later from my parents who visited me the following January. The last couple to receive the Christmas care package told my parents this story:

"My wife had to have major surgery the week before Christmas. Our lives were turned upside down. Celebrating Christmas was the farthest thing from our minds. I was exhausted from staying with her at the hospital every day and then coming home in the evenings to care for our two sons.

"The doctor discharged her on Christmas Eve. Of course we were grateful to have her back home, but the thought of bringing her to the neglected apartment and facing her recuperation drained what little strength I had left.

"We had no Christmas tree and no presents. It was a cold evening with a misty rain. I helped my wife carefully up the steps to our apartment. Nearing the door we noticed an oddly-shaped package on the floor. My eyes widened as I sniffed at an open corner of its wrappings. Wonderful! After settling her gently on our sofa, we raised the plate of Christmas goodies before us as if it were a rare treasure, an offering fit for a king.

"Our eyes met. Tears overflowed, running down our tired faces. Someone cares. Someone really cares! Isn't that what Christmas is all about?"

—Helen Hertha Kesinger

The Hanukkah Bush

Sixty-three Christmases have come and gone in my life, each with its own special flavor. But the one that stands out from all the rest is the Christmas of 1950. Stan and I had been married only seven months, and in our "leap first—look later" teenage marriage, many vital issues had never been discussed. How and where we would celebrate the major holidays called for mature decision-making skills which both of us lacked.

Stan's family didn't celebrate Christmas because they were still awaiting the birth of their Messiah and considered Jesus an impostor. Instead, they celebrated Hanukkah, the festival of lights with a traditional meal, the lighting of the Menorah and the spinning of the dreidel for gifts.

In my family, however, Christmas was the most important holiday of the year. It usually was a two-day affair with aunts and uncles sleeping on couches and rollaways; their children beside them on the floor. A miniature Victorian village was set up in the dining room on the buffet. In the living room the gateleg table held the large manger scene with each figure facing the Holy Infant; across the room the magnificent tree

stood blazing with lights on it's top almost brushing the ceiling. Gaily-wrapped gifts were piled half-way up its trunk. Add the aroma of roasted turkey, plum pudding, mince and pumpkin pies . . . delicious!

In my naiveté I believed nothing would ever change, but marriage brings many changes. I instituted the first change by suggesting that we spend Thanksgiving Day with Stan's family and the Christmas holidays with my family. My in-laws were delighted with what seemed a logical compromise. My mother was aghast that I would spend a major holiday with "strangers." She asked if perhaps we would like our Christmas gifts mailed to put under our own tree.

Stan said, "What do you mean 'our own tree?' That would break my Mother's heart if I put up a Christmas tree."

Now I was aghast and cried, "Do you mean now that I'm married to you, I can never celebrate Christmas again?"

"Not with a tree," he rejoined, "and that's final!"

I was devastated and begged, pleaded, wept, and cajoled for weeks—to no avail. One evening when Stan left to visit a friend, I thought of the endless succession of bleak Christmases to come and how sad that would be for any little children we might have. Through tears I managed to whisper, "Please Lord."

The phone rang. It was Stan's sister, Bette, and she explained that Stan

38

had come to their house instead of his friend's. The three of them (including brother-in-law, Lou) weighed the pros and cons of a Christmas tree and decided that love should be the determining factor.

"So," Bette continued, "we just bought your first Christmas tree and we'd all like to help decorate it."

What a wonderful evening! While I made hot cocoa and set out the cookies, they attacked the tree with gusto. What they lacked in expertise, they made up for in enthusiasm. They were crestfallen when I made them remove all the ornaments and put on the lights first, but they soon recovered in the sheer joy of tinsel-tossing. Finally they stood back to admire their work, and dubbed the little tree the "Hanukkah Bush."

Later my father-in-law made a six-pointed star out of strips of pine, covered it with aluminum foil and attached a blue Christmas tree light at each point. We hung it on the wall opposite the tree so we had the Star of David illuminating one corner and the "Hanukkah Bush" illuminating the other.

The real illumination in our home, though, was the Light of the world Who took up residence in our hearts and taught us how to love. If there is ever going to be "peace on earth and goodwill to men," it will have to start in families first as it did in ours on that Christmas so long ago.

—Betty Huff

39

Gabriel's Questions

Gabriel must have scratched his head at this one. He wasn't one to question his God-given missions. Sending fire and dividing seas were all in an eternity's work for this angel. When God sent, Gabriel went.

And when word got out that God was to become man, Gabriel was enthused. He could envision the moment:

The Messiah in a blazing chariot.
The King descending on a fiery cloud.
An explosion of light from which the Messiah would emerge.

That's what he expected. What he never expected, however, was what he got: a slip of paper with a Nazarene address. "God will become a baby," it read. "Tell the mother to name the child Jesus. And tell her not to be afraid."

Gabriel was never one to question, but this time he had to wonder.

God will become a baby? Gabriel had seen babies before. He had been platoon leader on the bulrush operation. He remembered what little Moses looked like.

40

That's okay for humans, he thought to himself. But God?

The heavens cannot contain him; how could a baby? Besides, have you seen what comes out of those babies? Hardly befitting for the Creator of the universe. Babies must be carried and fed, bounced and bathed. To imagine some mother burping God on her shoulder—why that was beyond what even an angel could imagine.

And what of this name—what was it—Jesus? Such a common name. There's a Jesus in every cul-de-sac. Come on, even Gabriel has more punch to it than Jesus. Call the baby Eminence or Majesty or Heaven-sent. Anything but Jesus.

So Gabriel scratched his head. What happened to the good ol' days? The Sodom and Gomorrah stuff. Flooding the globe. Flaming swords. That's the action he liked. But Gabriel had his orders. Take the message to Mary. Must be a special girl, he assumed as he traveled. But Gabriel was in for another shock. One peek told him Mary was not a queen. The mother-to-be of God was not regal. She was a Jewish peasant who'd barely outgrown her acne and had a crush on a guy named Joe.

And speaking of Joe—what does this fellow know? Might as well be a weaver in Spain or a cobbler in Greece. He's a carpenter. Look at him over there, sawdust in his beard and nail apron around his waist. You're

telling me God is going to have dinner every night with him? You're telling me the source of wisdom is going to call this guy "Dad?" You're telling me a common laborer is going to be charged with giving food to God?

What if he gets laid off?

What if he gets cranky?

What if he decides to run off with a pretty young girl from down the street? Then where will we be?

It was all Gabriel could do to keep from turning back. "This is a peculiar idea you have, God," he must have muttered to himself.

Are God's guardians given to such musings?

Are we? Are we still stunned by God's coming? Still staggered by the event? Does Christmas still spawn the same speechless wonder it did two thousand years ago?

I've been asking that question lately—to myself. As I write, Christmas is only days away and something just happened that has me concerned that the pace of the holidays may be overshadowing the purpose of the holidays.

I saw a manger in a mall. Correct that. I barely saw a manger in a

mall. I almost didn't see it. I was in a hurry. Guests coming. Santa dropping in. Sermons to be prepared. Services to be planned. Presents to be purchased.

The crush of things was so great that the crèche of Christ was almost ignored. I nearly missed it. And had it not been for the child and his father, I would have.

But out of the corner of my eye, I saw them. The little boy, three, maybe four years old, in jeans and high-tops staring at the manger's infant. The father, in baseball hat and work clothes, looking over his son's shoulder, gesturing first at Joseph, then Mary, then the baby. He was telling the little fellow the story.

And oh, the twinkle in the boy's eyes. The wonder on his little face. He didn't speak. He listened. And I didn't move. I just watched. What questions were filling the little boy's head? Could they have been the same as Gabriel's? What sparked the amazement on his face? Was it the magic?

And why is it that out of a hundred or so of God's children only two paused to consider his son? What is this December demon that steals our eyes and stills our tongues? Isn't this the season to pause and pose Gabriel questions?

The tragedy is not that we can't answer them, but that we are too busy to ask them.

Only heaven knows how long Gabriel fluttered unseen above Mary before he took a breath and broke the news. But he did. He told her the name. He told her the plan. He told her not to be afraid. And when he announced, "With God nothing is impossible!" he said as much for himself as for her.

For even though he couldn't answer the questions, he knew who could, and that was enough. And even though we can't answer them all, taking time to ask a few would be a good start.

—Max Lucado

44

A Christmas Blessing

I rested my hand on the gate and looked at the torn screen and crumbling chimney of the dilapidated house. A sudden gust of wind sent a crumpled paper rolling across the tall weeds and grass. I sighed as I tightened my grip on the pamphlets and the container in my hands.

"It would be useless to go there," I told myself. "All it would do is embarrass both of us."

I turned toward the house on the right and rehearsed my speech, moving toward it. A middle-aged lady dressed in a plaid skirt answered my knock.

"Merry Christmas," I said and handed her a pamphlet. "We're going door to door throughout various neighborhoods, asking for contributions to help needy families. Any donation which you can make will be most welcome." I smiled as I held out the collection can. She asked a few questions about the organization, then reached for her purse and dropped a dollar bill into the container.

"Thank you and have a happy holiday."

I stood on the sidewalk looking for my partner who was soliciting the houses across the street. I glanced back at the dilapidated house and

45

felt a strong urge to knock on the door.

Why am I doing this? I asked myself as I retraced my steps. They can't possibly contribute. But no matter how much I tried to dissuade myself, the urging persisted. I heard steps approaching in response to my knock.

"Mer . . . Merry Christmas," I stammered with embarrassment, as I looked at the lady wearing a shapeless gray dress. She held a whimpering baby in her arms, while several barefoot children of various heights huddled around her.

She nodded and murmured "Merry Christmas." Not knowing what else to say, I proceeded with my rehearsed speech.

"I'm sorry we don't have any money to give." She looked down at the child tugging at her dress, "but please come in and warm yourself. It's a cold night."

I took a step forward—forgetting the rule that stated we must never enter a house. With her free hand she cleared an area on the torn sofa and asked me to sit. The children immediately began competing with each other, vying for a spot next to me. The girl who sat on my right, began stroking the fabric of my coat, while the boy on my left took the pamphlets and began rifling through them.

"My husband lost his job several months ago. He finally found another one. Even though it's hard for him to work nights and sleep days, he's glad to be working again."

A little girl with brown curls and long eyelashes smiled shyly at me. She sat on her sister's lap and slipped her cold hand into mine.

"A lot of people are without jobs," I said, recalling my own struggle to find one after graduating from high school a few months earlier. "I'm glad your husband is working again," I said trying to sound cheerful.

She smiled and nodded. There seemed to be nothing more to say. I stood up, gathered the scattered pamphlets and waved to the children.

I stopped at several more houses before meeting up with my partner who was waiting at the corner. We drove to the church basement where we left our donations.

When I arrived home, I shared the experience with my mother. She offered to donate some canned goods from our pantry. The following weekend I baked cookies and asked some neighbors who had young children to donate clothes. I bought inexpensive toys, wrapped them and labeled them with the appropriate age.

On Christmas Eve, mom and I loaded her car with our precious bounty. The same lady encircled by the same group of children answered our knock. This time I didn't stammer as I said "Merry

47

Christmas." She invited us in and smiled as she accepted the boxes. The children followed her to the table and began reaching for the wrapped packages.

"Wait until tomorrow morning to open them. Daddy will be home then." She thanked us, wiped tears from her eyes and offered us a cup of coffee.

When we were ready to leave it occurred to me that we hadn't exchanged names. We introduced ourselves and invited her to our worship service.

The following Sunday, as I stood on the aisle looking for a place to sit, I felt a tug on my sleeve. I looked down. A little girl with brown curls and long eyelashes slipped her hand into mine.

I whispered a prayer thanking God that he had urged me to visit that dilapidated house.

—Pauline Jaramillo

48

Wrapping It Up Tips

• Wrap gifts as you buy them so it is never an overwhelming job on Christmas eve. This ensures you will use up your last year's left-over wrapping supplies first before you go out and buy too much new wrap now. Also, you will then have a better idea how much to purchase at after Christmas sales.

• Wrap each person's gifts all in one color or wrap so they are easily identifiable—especially for small children.

• Use unique wrap—comics, wallpaper leftovers, brown paper that you can use your stamps or stickers on.

• Run wrinkled ribbon through your curling iron. To renew wrinkled wrapping, lightly spray starch on the underside and iron.

• Consider fabric strips for bows on bags.

• When buying paper, consider red striped which can be used year round. I buy it by the yard at Tall Mouse or Michaels.

Decorate with Unusual Wrappings and Trims

• Deck out a hostess gift with tinsel and an ornament she can hang on her tree.

49

• Add artificial pine, real pine cones, holly, brass horn, bells, plaid ribbon and teddy bear ornament or cookie cutter.

• Tie up a home-sewers' present with pretty eyelet trim she'll use later on.

• Please a little girl with a streamer of hair ribbons to wear all year long.

• Guarantee a thank-you: Put a sprig of artificial mistletoe atop his tie box!

• Delight a gardener with a bright bunch of seed packets strung together.

• For those on your list who like to travel, wrap their gift in a large, colorful map. Tie it with a big red or green ribbon.

• Kitchen gifts look nice wrapped in a kitchen towel. A colored plastic or copper scouring pad can be your bow. Add colorful plastic measuring spoons. A wooden spoon can be your gift tag—tape their name right on the spoon.

—Sue Mellis

50

Where is the Child?

Many years ago a wealthy family decided to have their new-born baby baptized in their enormous mansion. Dozens of guests were invited to the elaborate affair, and they all arrived dressed in the latest fashion. After depositing their elegant wraps on a bed in an upstairs room, the guests were entertained royally. Soon the time came for the main purpose of their gathering, the infant's baptismal ceremony. But where was the child? No one seemed to know.

The child's governess ran upstairs, only to return with a desperate look on her face. Everyone searched frantically for the baby. Then, someone recalled having seen the child sleeping on one of the beds. The baby was on a bed, all right—buried underneath a pile of coats, jackets and furs. The very object of that day's celebration had been forgotten, neglected, and nearly smothered.

I can't help but remember that story as I walk along busy city streets during this holiday season. Everywhere I look I see lights, tinsel, trimmings and trappings and shoppers loaded down with

expensive gifts that may take the next year to pay off. And I ask myself, "Is this Christmas?"

Where is the Child whose birthday we celebrate?

During the first Christmas, wise men from the East came to the city of Bethlehem, looking for the Christ Child. They came searching for One who would become the Savior of the world. Today, if we were to search for Jesus in the homes and streets of our towns and cities, would we find Him?

—Luis Palau

52

My Amanda

As the organist softly played carols, husband Howard and I settled ourselves in church. I glanced at the bulletin and my eyes stopped at the notation: "Dolls, toys, citrus fruit, nuts and candy are urgently requested for the Christmas party for needy children."

At the mention of dolls, I thought of Amanda, my doll as big as a one-year-old baby, safely cradled away in an old trunk for many years. I'd received her during The Depression, that lean year on the farm when my parents sacrificed to buy us the one gift of our choice from the ragged Sears Roebuck catalog. I pushed the thought of Amanda out of my mind as I tried to concentrate on the sermon, but my eyes returned again and again to that notice.

"How foolish!" I fretted to myself. No little girl would love my old doll— even my own four daughters hadn't wanted her. Girls today want dolls that have hair to wash and comb, or dolls that can wet, walk, talk, blow a kiss, or even roller-skate. All Amanda could do was smile her sweet smile with her two little pearl teeth showing and close her eyes when laid down.

"Let's send a check to buy something for the needy children's

53

Christmas," I said on the way home from church.

"Go ahead," Howard agreed. "It's a good idea. It's almost like giving Jesus a birthday gift. Remember that Scripture verse, *Inasmuch as ye have done it unto one of the least of these my brethren, ye have done it unto me* (Matthew 25:40)."

I nodded. "I'll mail a check in the morning."

Monday I dropped a check into the mail. But I thought, "Some little girl who wants a doll might not get one."

I finally admitted to myself, "I guess I don't want to give Amanda to a strange little girl. No one could love and take good care of Amanda like I did. She'd been my best friend when I had no one else to play with."

Almost against my will, my feet marched me to the storeroom where the old trunk stood against the far wall. I unloaded the boxes piled on top and lifted the lid. There lay Amanda, asleep for what had now been many years. To me she still looked beautiful and lovable. I remembered again the Christmas morning I received her. There under the tree sat a doll as big as my baby brother. The doll was dressed in a pink organdy dress and bonnet. "My Amanda," I'd whispered. The joy she gave me must have warmed my parents' hearts.

Years later I packed Amanda away when I entered nurses training. She'd been out from time to time as my daughters grew. But they

ignored her; so I returned her to the trunk. Now Amanda's closed lashes rested on her rosy cheeks, and I thought again of my husband's remark, "like giving Jesus a birthday gift."

I picked Amanda up, and immediately her crystal blue eyes popped open. Impulsively I whispered, "Amanda, would you like to be adopted by a new little girl— one who would play with you every day and love you like I did so long ago?"

Amanda smiled her little open-mouthed smile as if to say, "Oh, yes, please!"

I carried her into the house and took off her wrinkled clothes which smelled of moth balls. They needed washing. "I'll make you look like new, Amanda," I promised.

As I ironed, I relived other holidays when my mother made Amanda a new dress or bonnet or bought a tiny pair of soft shoes, knowing that gift would please me more than anything.

That day Amanda and I spent together was memorable. I redressed her in the freshly starched dress and bonnet and tiny anklets that covered the little broken toe I'd cried about so many years ago— over fifty— could it be? I recalled what a tragedy it seemed then. Her wounded toe was the only indication that she was "used."

I walked to the car, still not sure I could follow through with this

love gift. I sat Amanda on the seat beside me and drove slowly to the mission headquarters where they collected the donations. Carefully picking up Amanda, I strode inside. I hid my moist eyes as I handed her to someone at the mission and turned to leave. It was almost a prayer, "Let some little girl love Amanda as much as I did." I knew God was aware of the emotional struggle in my heart, even though I'd never know the answer.

I felt good, yet thoughtful, after I came home. Later my husband asked, "Why are you so quiet this evening?"

I smiled and kissed him. I wasn't sure he'd understand.

Christmas morning, even in the midst of our own family get together, I remembered Amanda and my heart sang in the hope that she'd been welcomed by a girl that was as happy today as I'd been as a child.

Months later we attended a missionary meeting at church and saw movies taken at the children's Christmas party. There on the screen I saw a long table of dolls, and in the midst, much bigger than the others, sat my Amanda!

I caught my breath. Suddenly I saw a line of little girls choosing the doll she wanted. As I watched, a pair of arms reached up and clasped Amanda and held her tenderly like a real baby. Then I knew— Amanda would find love in her new home.

—Mary Lou Klingler

Seasonal Seesaw

I am a Christmas contradiction. I'm up with excitement and then down with disappointment. I'm up with anticipation and then down with depression. I'm up with . . . well, you get the idea. I'm on my seasonal seesaw. My teeter-totter partner is my own Currier-and-Ives expectations.

Ever notice in those Currier and Ives pictures how even in frigid weather the cows are contented? They willingly pose next to the wood for the fireplace, which is neatly stacked next to the house. While Bossy grins, Junior is shown joyfully skipping out to bring Mother dear kindling for the stove.

I don't have a cow, but I do have a dog. Pumpkin refuses to go outside if it's damp. She has an aversion to moist feet. She will sit for days with her paws crossed, waiting for the sun or wind to dry up the ground. No way is she going to willingly pose by a wet wood pile.

Of course, that would be difficult, since we don't have wood—that is, unless I hike five miles to the woods and gnaw off a few branches. Oh, well, our fireplace stays cleaner that way.

I tried to imagine our Junior joyfully skipping toward a task outside

in inclement weather. Ha! I think Junior caught Pumpkin's malady.

No matter how I try, I can't seem to cram my family onto the front of one of those cards.

I don't know why I can't remember, from one Christmas season to the next, that Currier and Ives is an unattainable height. Every Christmas, I want my house to be picture-perfect. Ha! I can't achieve that in a nonholiday time, much less in a season with so many added demands.

I imagine white birch logs (cut by me in our back 40—feet, that is) snuggled in a handwoven basket (I designed) placed next to the hearth. The blazing fire invites guests to warm in our candle-lit (all hand-dipped by yours truly) dining room. I would serve a gourmet dinner for 30, followed by strolling musicians playing Handel's *Messiah*. All this would take place in my 10-by-12 dining area.

One year we decided to write Noel in lights on our house. We started late and finished only half the project because of bad weather. That left a multi-colored "NO" flashing on our rooftop. We had fewer guests that year.

Also, during the holiday hoopla I seem to get bit by the bug. No, not the flu bug; the love bug. I fall into the trap of thinking everyone is

going to get along. Give me a break! How unrealistic to believe relatives and friends, some of whom have never hit it off, would suddenly become seasonal sidekicks! I'm learning that there are those who believe "Ho, Ho, Ho" is something you do strictly in your garden and has nothing to do with exhibiting a merry heart.

Another habit I have is wanting everyone to love the gifts I give them as much as I did when I selected them. I'm into applause and appreciation. Here's the problem: I live with three guys (one husband and two sons), and they only applaud silly things like grand-slam home runs in the World Series, touchdowns in the final seconds of the Super Bowl, or when I fix dinner and they can tell what it is.

They don't show the same enthusiasm for my gifts—like the nifty button extenders, monogrammed electric socks, or fuchsia-colored long johns I wrapped for them. I realize my gifts are...uh...distinctive, but I want them to be memorable. My guys agree they have been.

Well, there it is, my Christmas confession. Maybe some of you can identify with part, if not all, of my seasonal seesaw. Come join me in entering into the holidays without the teeter and totter in our emotions.

—Patsy Clairmont

59

Gift Ideas for Children

Leave "Santa notes" in each stocking with little reminders of the past year (i.e. how proud you are of them or what great things they have done that you want to remember).

Wrap children's gifts with a thought as to how they will be unwrapped. A glued, stapled-shut box or impenetrable strapping tape or plastic bags all have great frustration potential. Don't let the container ruin the fun of the gift. Maybe no wrapping is really needed and a bow will do fine.

If something needs batteries, have them in place and ready to go. It is frustrating to have something that is supposed to move, play or be automated in some way and not have the power available.

Allow children to open gifts at their own pace. Some presents are real show-stoppers and should be allowed to do that.

Give the gift of "time" for that special child during this season. There is certainly a value to quality time, but there is also great merit in quantity time we make available to children.

Use this season to teach the sharing of gifts with children. Perhaps a toy could be chosen to give to someone in need. You might be surprised at their choice.

Buy each member of your family at least one practical gift that will only be opened when the tree is untrimmed after the holiday. Hide each present in a different place in the house. Tuck clues to the gift hunt in the branches of the tree. This is a great hint to help with the job of undecorating. Remember, decorating is always much more fun than undecorating.

—Martha Baker

Christmas Tree Fun

We decorated six trees each Christmas: a large one for the living room and five small ones for each child's room. The children would each have to create their decorations and put them on their trees. We all gathered in the living room to decorate the big tree together. Then I inspected all the trees and awarded prizes for the most beautiful, most original, most colorful, most heartwarming, most unusual, etc.

As you can guess, everyone got a prize.

—Art Linkletter

61

Christmas Far From Home

The wind-driven snow stung my cheeks with icy particles that felt like tiny slivers of glass as I hurried to gather the diapers from the clothesline. I glanced over at the nearby shack where a family of five, soon to be six, lived in two small rooms. The wind was tearing at the tarpaper siding on their home and blowing the smoke from the stovepipe in a horizontal plume. I wondered if they were staying warm.

It was not yet Christmas, but already my first winter in this "southern" state of Arkansas seemed much colder than what I had known back home in Montana. I hurried inside with my armload of laundry to warm up beside the tiny heating stove but it couldn't take away my homesickness.

We were barely into the second year of World War II and my husband was stationed at an air base in this country. I hated the barren little house with so few conveniences. No indoor plumbing, no central heating, not even curtains. As I started folding Jimmy's diapers, I glanced at the scrawny little Christmas tree standing in the corner. My husband's paycheck didn't stretch far enough to buy more than a single string of lights for the tree. I remembered other

Christmases in my parents' home. The huge Christmas tree, with presents piled high around it, reached all the way to the ceiling.

A knock at the door interrupted my reverie. As I opened the door, I immediately recognized the three small children who lived in the tarpaper shack behind my house.

"Please, ma'am," the eldest girl was saying, "may we come in and look at your Christmas tree? We saw the pretty lights through the window."

As they trooped inside and I closed the door behind them, an appreciative "oooh" went up from them simultaneously. The eldest squeezed her little sister's hand and whispered, "Isn't it beautiful?"

The tree that only moments before had seemed so scrawny and inadequate now took on a new dignity, a new beauty. I was sure these little 'tykes' didn't have a Christmas tree in their home. Jimmy woke up and the children gathered around his crib to admire him. I thought of how the shepherds, their faces also shining with awe, had gathered around another Babe long ago.

After the children left, I sat rocking Jimmy and thinking about the little girls and their parents. Their father had a disabling lung condition and couldn't work. Their mother had very limited vision.

She received a small "blind pension." It was all they had to live on.

By the next morning, I had reached a decision. My destitute neighbors would not go hungry on Christmas Day if I could help it. Bundling Jimmy up in warm clothes, I went from house to house in the neighborhood, asking people I had not met before to contribute to a food basket for our needy neighbors. As often happens when folks are made aware of a need, they responded generously. There was enough food, not only for a fine Christmas dinner, but to make nourishing meals for several weeks to come. With some of the money I had saved to spend on gifts for Jimmy and my husband, I bought three pair of bright warm mittens to cover the cold hands of the girls. And then, in a wave of generosity, I also purchased three coloring books and a box of crayons.

It was while I was selecting the coloring books that I overheard two women talking about a Christmas program that would be presented that night at a nearby church. I hadn't attended church since moving to Arkansas, but suddenly it was something I wanted to do.

That night, as I washed the dishes, I glanced out of the window and saw my neighbors' small home and wondered, "The greatest

gift I can give those three little girls is an opportunity to learn the true meaning of Christmas."

Their parents seemed pleased when I asked if the girls could go to the Christmas program with us. As we entered the beautifully-decorated church, the children's eyes grew wide with wonder. They watched, totally enthralled, as the Sunday School students re-enacted the story of Christ's birth.

Walking home in the crisp night air, a small mittened hand in my own, I looked up at the stars twinkling in the velvet sky. Tears of joy welled up in my eyes as I realized that this was really Christmas. It didn't matter that I was far from where I had always celebrated Christmas. It didn't matter that things were not the same.

What really mattered was the peace and love that filled my heart, the awareness of the Lord's presence.

"Thank you, God," I whispered.

—Roberta Donovan

65

Picture-Perfect Decorations?

It's nearing Christmastime and the department stores are gilded with magazine-perfect holiday decorations. Take a look at the Christmas trees. See that one? It must have come straight from the forest, heaped with flocking (or is it snow?), little birds grasping the branches, pine cones hanging from the boughs, and the unmistakable scent of pine wafting about the nostrils? And that one over there is a child's dream with little wooden ornaments of every child's favorite toys. Ah, there's a display with the ever-popular Victorian styling. Ribbons and bows, fans, crystal ornaments, wreaths, all color-coordinated. Gorgeous, aren't they?

Eyes closed, I imagine them in my living room . . . and chuckle. My household's decorations share no resemblance to these photogenic beauties. I think of our tree with no obvious theme and few matching ornaments, most of them hand-made from egg cartons, bottle tops, plastic lids, yam, and a conglomeration of left-over materials. Our decorations? The same, a recycled menagerie. Hardly picture-perfect, but then history seldom is.

66

Our history. Each year we revisit it when we ceremoniously carry out "the box" and pull out the decorations one by one.

We start with the ornaments. "Mom, isn't it about time we dump these?" my preteens ask, holding up the egg carton ornaments, which have lost most of their glitter and appear ready to fall apart. "Not those, kiddos," and I launch into the story.

It was 1979 in Seattle, our first Christmas as newlyweds, and the coldest winter in 70 years. Daddy couldn't work because the ground was too frozen. We didn't have much money, but we were happy. I knitted him a scarf to wear on those bitter cold mornings, and he had scraped enough pennies together to buy me a wrought-iron plant stand for my green-leafed children. A Christmas tree? Who needed one? We had each other and the Christ of Christmas in our hearts. That was enough.

Two days before Christmas, unexpected visitors knocked at the door. There stood three children from our church with a parent in tow. They came in and set up a small tree boasting handmade ornaments of egg carton sections and glitter. We chorused together and hugged the children who reminded us that some day we'd have our own children with which to share such moments.

"Hey, here's one of mine!" Rachel, the youngest, squeals with embarrassment. "I made this in kindergarten!" She stares at the back-side of the handmade angel which sports her name, a date, and photo. Everybody laughs at how "cute" she is.

Holly, her older sister, holds an ornament and her face brightens. "This is one I made in third grade. That's the year I met Kathy." She remembers meeting Kathy "that annoying girl in the green dress with pink flowers," who would eventually become her best friend for seven years.

Then there are the ornaments which go beyond our own experiences like the glass bulbs passed down from my great-grandmother the family matriarch.

The angel is placed last. "It's Nancy's angel!" D.J., our oldest, exclaims. The kids reminisce about how she babysat them while I went to the hospital, even though we'd never met her before. Our friendship grew and now the angel reminds us of God's help in times of need.

The stockings are lifted out next. "This one's getting pretty dirty," my husband Doug says. But it's a stocking I had had since birth. It gets hung right beside the new ones.

Last are the "famous" works of art to hang on the walls. Well,

"famous" to us. The nativity scene Holly colored in Sunday School made it obvious even then that we had a budding artist in our midst. We hang up creations hand-crafted at school, at church, and at home.

Our handiwork completed, we sit and admire our transformed room. These walls will never adorn the cover of *Good Housekeeping* or *Saturday Evening Post*, but they don't need to. Our mismatched, non-thematic decorations are a piece of true Americana.

Picture-perfect? Hardly. But they're ours.

—Jami C. Lewis

69

Just A Tiny Stall

Everything would have been fine if I hadn't gotten lost on our way home and gone three hours out of the way. So my two daughters and I arrived too late to keep our reservations at the motel and were forced to travel on into the night searching for another one.

It was raining heavily. The oncoming headlights glaring up from the slickened highway burned my tired eyes and made my head ache.

"Mommy, I'm sleepy," Tammy, my five-year-old said in a tiny voice.

"Me, too," eight-year-old Dawn grumbled. "When are we going to be home?"

"We won't be home until tomorrow" I explained, "but we will be able to sleep as soon as we come to the next exit."

I turned off the big highway, pulled up to the first motel we cameto and went inside to register.

"Sorry Ma'am," the young girl behind the desk told us, "I rented the last room a half an hour ago."

70

My shoulders slumped. I was so tired, the very thought of traveling further frightened me. I couldn't let the girls know how worried I was, so with a tired smile I said, "Come along girls. We'll find another place to stay."

But the next three motels were full also and we were forced to continue our journey. It was 1:30 a.m. and the girls were curled up sound asleep. It was then I prayed a small but fervent prayer. I knew with confidence the Lord had heard and would answer.

On the outskirts of the next town was a tiny building displaying a rather crude sign "ROOMS FOR THE NIGHT." Several of the lights surrounding the words were burned out, but my lights bounced off it as I exited the main highway. My throbbing head and heavy eyes wouldn't let me drive past.

"Are we home?" Dawn asked anxiously, rubbing her sleepy eyes.

"No," I answered shaking my head wearily. "We're going to see if they have a room." As we crawled out into the night, the cold rain hitting my face snapped me awake. We entered the door marked "Office" and stood at the chest-high desk where a bell boasted, "Ring for service."

I almost didn't ring it thinking, "Why bother the owner at this

hour? They won't have a room anyway." But feeling desperate, I rang the bell loudly, and watched as a sleepy-eyed, gray-haired old man tottered up to the desk.

"Well, well, young lady, so you need a room do you?" He questioned with a friendly grin. "You all look very tired, and hungry too. Have you traveled far?"

"It seems like it," I answered weakly.

"Okay, why don't you go to your room and get settled in? In the meantime, I'll have Millie rustle up something for you in the kitchen."

"You mean you have a room?" I sighed gratefully.

"Got lots of 'em. Not many folks stop here anymore since they got all those fancy places down the road. All we have to offer here are clean sheets and good food. Now, you and your young'uns run along and I'll get Millie to start cooking."

"Oh, you don't need to fix anything," I began.

"Millie loves to do for others and hasn't had much call to do so lately. It'll please her," he smiled.

"Thank You, Lord," I whispered gratefully as I ran toward the car to get the suitcases.

He showed us our room and said in a gentle tone, "I'll knock on the door when the food's ready."

"Oh, boy, you mean we're finally going to eat?" Dawn asked happily. "I'm starved!" After we had eaten and returned to our room, I was tucking the girls into bed when Tammy said, "Mommy, this is just like the Jesus story, isn't it?"

"Oh, really?" I questioned curiously. "How's that?"

"Well, we traveled a long way like His mommy and daddy did. We were tired, cold and hungry and couldn't find a place to stay either." She smiled up at me. "But now we are safe and warm. Goodnight Mommy." She snuggled into the clean sheets and closed her eyes.

Yes, our experience was a lot like the story of long ago. How tired Mary must have been as she made the trip on that donkey. How discouraging for Joseph when every inn was full. I'm sure they, like we, were most grateful for the tiny nook without frills.

I crawled into bed wiping the tears from my eyes and whispering a prayer of thanks for the tiny "stall" we shared.

—Marcia Krugh Leaser

73

Looking to the Cross at Christmas

Legend has it that long ago a small, insignificant plant once grew wild on the hillsides outside of Jerusalem. The flowers were so tiny they went unnoticed, that is, until the day Christ was crucified.

One of these small plants grew near the base of Christ's cross. As Christ hung there bleeding, his blood dropped down upon the top leaves of the little bush. As more of his blood fell the leaves became permanently stained, transforming the bush into a beautiful new creation.

Since all eyes were directed upward toward Christ the bush initially captured no one's attention. But as Christ was taken down from the cross one of his followers, a young lady took note of it. She had never seen such a beautifully unique red bush. Her heart was touched. She took it home with her as a reminder of Christ shedding his blood, like the innocent sacrificial lamb at the temple.

Other believers in Christ quickly learned of the plant and wanted one of their own. It was discovered when the conditions were right it easily took root; just as Christ does in our hearts. When broken the plant bled, not red but white, representing the purity of Christ's sacrifice.

74

The flower and its surrounding red leaves fade away. Although they revive when the darkness of the night lengthens. This commemorates the dark day Christ died. Its color bursts forth in brightness, as Christ burst forth from the tomb. He gained victory over death—having paid our debt with his blood.

The poinsettia reminds us of the real reason we celebrate Christ's coming to this world as an innocent child. It points us to the cross and the empty tomb.

—Tamera Easterday

75

The Flight to Egypt

A few years ago, a friend of mine was teaching Sunday School to young children. It was around Christmastime and they had been studying about the birth of Jesus and the events surrounding it.

My friend was telling the children about the flight to Egypt taken from Matthew 2. She asked them to draw a picture of this story and turn them in at the end of the class time.

When the pictures were handed in, the teacher was looking them over and complimenting each child on their work. She came to one picture which puzzled her. Most of the children had drawn a picture of Mary and Joseph with baby Jesus riding on camels or donkeys. But this particular picture showed an airplane which had four people in it.

My friend asked the little artist, who happened to be very knowledgeable in Bible matters, to explain her picture. She eagerly replied, "Yes! That's baby Jesus, Mary and Joseph." My friend asked who the fourth person in the picture was, and the little girl exclaimed, "Oh! That's Pontius the pilot!"

—Lynette S. McBride

A Cup of Christmas

Christmas is a special time for friends and family to gather together, and a Christmas tea offers a wonderful chance to celebrate your relationships and the season itself. Let your "Cup of Christmas" tea be your special holiday gift to your friends, your family, and yourself.

Start early to plan your tea so you can approach your celebration with serenity instead of panic. (I always begin planning in October for a mid-December tea.) Find beautiful Christmas-theme note cards with no message inside to use for invitations. And have fun when it comes to planning the decor and menu of the Christmas season offers so many wonderful possibilities. Take full advantage of all the wonderful decorating materials that are available— sparkling red-and-green fabrics, lush and fragrant greens, all kinds of candles. Load your table with a groaning variety of sweet and savory foods. And let your holiday message be one of abundant good cheer and memories in the making.

77

Almost any "Christmas party" food lends itself to tea-party fare. I like to take advantage of rich flavors and wonderful ingredients.

Spiced Russian Tea
Southern Pecan Cake
Fresh Blackberries or Other Fruit
Marscarpone or Brie
Assorted Christmas Cookies

End your time together by singing carols around the fire or reading aloud from a Christmas classic, O'Henry's *The Gift of the Magi*, for example, or Tom Hegg's *A Cup of Christmas Tea.* The Christmas story from the Gospel of Luke is the perfect way to put the whole season in perspective!

SPICED RUSSIAN TEA

Russian tea was originally imported to Russia from China by camel caravan and traditionally served from a samovar or large tea urn. Russians drink their tea with lots of lemon and sugar, but no milk.

78

6 teaspoons Russian blend or any good black tea

1 pinch cloves

11/2 pints freshly boiled water

Place tea and cloves in pot. Add water, and brew for five minutes
   before pouring. Add sugar and lemon to taste.

SOUTHERN PECAN CAKE

This wonderful flourless cake was served at a Christmas tea in
the home of Susan Vineyard of Portland, Oregon. Everyone loved it!

2 cups pecans (very fresh)

5 large eggs, separated

2/3 cup sugar

1 teaspoon vanilla or 1 tablespoon cognac

Preheat oven to 325 degrees and grease and flour an 8-inch
springform pan. Roughly chop 1 1/2 cup pecans; set aside. Finely
chop the remaining pecans; add to other nuts. (A food processor
makes the chopping process much easier.) Beat the egg yolks in a
large bowl until they are lightly fluffed, add sugar and beat hard
until the mixture turns a lighter shade of yellow and is smooth.
Gently fold in nuts with a rubber spatula, add vanilla or cognac and

mix well. Beat egg whites until stiff but not dry. With a rubber spatula gently fold a third of the egg whites into the nut mixture to lighten it, then fold in the remaining egg whites. Spoon batter into prepared pan; it should be no more than 3/4 full. Place the pan on the middle shelf of the oven and bake 50 to 60 minutes, or until cake springs back when lightly touched. Cool in pan for 5 minutes, then run a thin knife around the sides to loosen the cake. Unclamp the pan and let cake cool completely before removing it from the bottom of the pan. Coat top and sides with Dark Sweet Chocolate Frosting. Makes 6 to 8 servings.

DARK SWEET CHOCOLATE FROSTING

8 ounces dark sweet chocolate
(Tobler's, Lindt, or Callebout)
1 cup heavy cream
Break chocolate into coarse pieces and melt in double boiler over barely simmering water. Add cream and stir until smooth. Remove the pan from heat and beat hard. Place in the refrigerator to firm up (about 30 minutes). Frost cake in a swirl design.

—Emilie Barnes

Our Prayer Basket

Taking down Christmas decorations each year is the only part of the holiday that I do not look forward to. The house always looks so bare after being filled all month long with bright red and green decorations, shining lights and glittering tinsel. There is a certain drabness that seems to reappear each January as each bulb is taken off the now-sagging tree.

A kind of sadness has always lingered in my heart during these undecorating sessions; a sadness that stems from the sinking feeling that I'm removing Christ from my home as I remove the post-Christmas clutter. I have always loved Christmas because of what it signifies— the celebration of our Savior's birth. The reminder is vivid during the Christmas season with all of the festive decor adorning our home; but it is too suddenly faded with each item packed away in an attic-bound box. It was during one such post-holiday teardown that a new year-long Christmas tradition began at our house.

I was lingering over the basket of Christmas cards sent from friends and relatives, reading them one last time before depositing them in the trash. It seems such a waste to throw these away, I thought. This is the only time of year I hear from some of these people and I feel so discon-

81

nected from them once I throw these cards away. Hand-poised over the kitchen garbage can, I suddenly remembered an idea I had heard from a woman who kept her Christmas cards all year long and then prayed for the people who sent them.

"Honey," I rushed into the living room to where my husband was de-tangling Christmas lights, "I have an idea that will keep Christmas alive in our home all year long!" "Does it include these lights?" he remarked sarcastically. "Because if it does, forget it; they're a mess!" I laughed at his attempt to smooth over what he knew was a difficult time for me. "No, all we need is this basket of cards," I said smiling.

That is how our prayer basket began. Each year as we take down our lights and tinsel, we put out our prayer basket in a prominent place, filled with Christmas cards that we received the previous season. Then, each Sunday we pick a new card from the basket and pray all week long for the one(s) who sent it. We make it a family event, and mealtime is a good time for everyone to participate. As we pray for the sender of each card, we are reminded of Christ's birth and its significance in our lives all year. Sometimes, we even send a short note at each week's end, letting the person or family know that we prayed for them for an entire week. The response can be heartwarming. And it's a wonderful way to keep Christ's love burning in our hearts all year.

—Laura Sabin Riley

Decorating Ideas

• Keep a roll of masking tape handy. As you receive cards, mount them on the door or a wall area in the shape of a Christmas tree.

• Memory decoration: Each year buy or make a tree decoration for your children, to be presented to them for their first tree.

• Christmas linens: Each year purchase or make one item to add to your collection.

• Decorate the front door as a reminder of the Holiday we celebrate. A wreath with a nativity scene tucked in the center or a banner with a Christmas motif will send a message to every visitor.

• Inside the entry of your home is a good place for a nativity scene.

• Buy several poinsettia plants early. Use them to decorate the house . . . then a day or two before Christmas give them away.

• Decorate the doors inside your house.

• Use luminaries to line your walk when guests are coming over.

• Freshen pine cone wreaths with hair spray.

• Plan a special place in your home to display your Advent Wreath.

—Martha Baker

83

The Angel Tree

Sharon was outraged. Several minutes had passed as she stood behind the woman who picked over the angels on the Christmas tree.

Every year the church collected names of needy children. Each one was represented by an angel on a Christmas tree in the foyer of the church. In the weeks preceding Christmas, members of the congregation chose angels for whom they would buy gifts.

Sharon had decided to join the church and she was feeling quite charitable. This would be her first act of kindness as a member. Who would God select for her to bless?

As she neared the tree, she was dismayed to see a woman picking over the angels, rejecting one after another. "No, I don't want this one. It's a ten-year-old boy who wants sports equipment. I don't know a thing about footballs and such." She pushed that angel aside and looked at another. "Here's a little girl who wants a dress. Forget it, dresses are so expensive these days," the woman objected.

What kind of a giving spirit is that? Sharon thought. She clenched her teeth as she waited for the lady to make a decision and leave. Finally, the woman took an angel of her liking and exited.

84

I'm going to trust God to select the right angel for me, Sharon thought with righteous indignation. In fact, I think I'll take two. She snatched two angels from the tree without reading them, shoved them in her pocket, and hurried away. She had never trusted God so sincerely before.

She rushed to the car where her husband, Arnold, awaited. "Who is our Angel?" he asked.

"Actually, I took two. The lady in front of me was so selective on who she was willing to buy for, I felt led to take two." She pulled the angels from her pocket.

"The first one is an eight-year-old boy who wants a football."

"Oh, that's easy." Arnold pulled the car into traffic thinking how easy this giving thing was going to be.

"The second one is . . . " Sharon gasped, "A dormitory of twenty-four fourteen-year-old girls."

"Oh, my goodness," Arnold looked for a place to pull off the road. "Do you want to take it back and change it for another angel?"

Sharon was reminded of the indignation she felt when the other lady picked over the angels she didn't want. Hadn't Sharon trusted the Lord to give her the ones He selected especially for her?

"No, I couldn't. This is what God wants me to do."

In the following two weeks, Sharon gathered up twenty-four shoe boxes and took them to the school where she worked. She explained what they were for and invited all the staff to join in the fun of filling them with make-up, earrings, combs, mirrors, and all sorts of things fourteen-year-old girls would love. When the boxes were full, Sharon wrapped them in beautiful paper and took them to the church for delivery. When she walked away from the church her spirit was renewed.

There would be an eight-year-old boy and twenty-four fourteen-year-old girls who would receive gifts. But more important, Sharon, Arnold, and many others were blessed by their obedience in giving.

—Karen Robertson

86

A Family's Holiday Double Standard

A Christmas get-together about thirty years ago showed me how the adults' double-standard for family holiday behavior looks to their youngsters.

Riding to my parents' home on Christmas morning, I warned four-year-old Bruce, "Now don't be rowdy and noisy, running all over the house. Play quietly so that everyone can enjoy the day."

Bruce took it to heart, as did his little sister, Becky. They mostly watched the antics of others. Here is what they saw during the day:

My sisters, brothers, their spouses and children were also there. We spread throughout the rooms, talking and laughing. Soon we concentrated in the living room, sampling sweet treats. My weight-conscious brother, following his usual dreaded rite, set the bathroom scales in our midst, inviting everyone to weigh in. People almost trampled each other, disappearing faster than the Christmas candies had.

Two-year-old Becky always asked Bruce to interpret events. "Where go, Bruce?"

The women gathered in the kitchen, preparing dinner with bursts of talk and laughter. My husband grabbed his camera and headed for the

87

kitchen. When the ladies caught sight of him, they mixed and milled like kids on a playground, trying to hide themselves. After following their Dad through the door, my kids quickly escaped.

Two young cousins conned the crowds, playing the men against the women as the children offered sheets of merchandise from which people could order to benefit school organizations. There was heavy traffic through the house to compare notes with spouses and get money for purchases. Bruce and Becky watched in wonder.

Later, at the dinner table, jokes and the retelling of funny family incidents caused some adults to bend low over the table as they muffled screams and hid their faces, contorted with mirth. Others rocked back and forth with loud laughter.

"What doin', Bruce?" Becky asked worriedly.

An older boy who had wangled a seat at the big table went into a fit of shouting merriment and suddenly fell backward, arms and legs flailing. He barely missed the children's table as he crashed. Wordless, Becky blanched and clung to Bruce.

After dinner, women constantly traversed the rooms, stridently topping each other's amplification. Men drifted outdoors, then stomped their feet heavily as they came in through the door. Animated

talk, loud laughter and calling between groups kept decibels high. Sets of children huddled about, playing relatively quiet games.

Finally, everyone began leaving with loud calls to each other as car motors roared and doors slammed.

Traveling home that evening, a sleepy Bruce asked me The Question: "Mom, how come I can't be noisy and rowdy and run all over the house, but all of you can?"

—Anita Heistand

The Story Behind
"O Little Town of Bethlehem"

Philips Brooks, a Boston bachelor and Philadelphia preacher wrote the words for this hymn in 1868 as a poem for children. While teaching Sunday school after the horrors of the Civil War, Brooks longed to impart the peace he had experienced on a journey through the Holy Land. In 1865 he had ridden on horseback from Jerusalem to Bethlehem and nearby fields—the resting place of shepherds who watched their flocks by night. That evening, he attended a worship service at the Ancient Church of the Nativity, built by Constantine in 326 on the site that tradition says is where Jesus was born. Brooks marveled at how God could come to earth in such a quiet, lowly way. But how to pass on his awe to others?

A poem didn't seem like enough. Brooks asked Lewis Redner, the church organist, to set his words to music so the children could sing it for a Christmas service. But Redner struggled to find a fitting tune. The more he wrestled, the worse it seemed until the night before the service there still was no melody.

90

Weary and discouraged, Redner went to bed. He felt he had disappointed his friend Brooks, the children, himself and God.

Sometime in the night a sweet angelic melody broke through his fog of sleep. God was speaking. Redner sprang from bed to jot down the notes, fitting them to Brooks' words until dawn: "Our hopes and fears of all the years . . . will rest in Thee tonight."

Christmas morning, he taught the 36 children and 6 teachers the new song. The hymn became so popular that when Brooks, who never married or had children of his own, died at age 58, the nation mourned. But one of his five-year-old friends, a devoted Sunday school student, said knowingly, "Oh Mother, how happy the angels will be."

—Melissa Wilson

91

Emmitt's Favorite

This is my husband's favorite pie. Christmas wouldn't be Christmas without it! Leave some room for this pie. It is really rich!

Part 1:
- 2 cups powdered sugar
- 1 stick oleo
- 1 8-ounce package cream cheese
- 2 egg whites
- 1 teaspoon vanilla

Soften oleo and cream cheese. Add other ingredients. Beat these ingredients at high speed on your mixer for ten minutes. Spread mixture in bottom of two baked and cooled pie shells.

Emmitt's Favorite

Part 2:
1 can crushed pineapple, well drained
2 packages Dream Whip
2 tablespoons powdered sugar
1 envelope unflavored gelatin
1 cup chopped pecans

Drain pineapple. Set aside. Prepare Dream Whip following directions on package. Beat in powdered sugar and unflavored gelatin. Reserve 1 cup of Dream Whip for top of two pies. Fold crushed pineapple, nuts and remaining Dream Whip. Pour into shells. Top with more Dream Whip.

This recipe is for two pies. Believe me, they will disappear fast!

—Joan Clayton

93

Corrie's Christmas Memories

It was Christmas, 1944. Betsie and I celebrated Christmas in Holland. We worked like a real team and often were the speakers at eight or ten Christmas feasts. In clubs, Sunday schools, hospitals, military groups, and churches—whenever we got a chance.

The Christmas treats were usually the same Christmas bread with powdered sugar on it and raisins. There was an orange for every child, too. At that time there were no sweet ones in the whole of Holland, and I still remember the sour taste! But it was a joy—a special Christmas joy. Then a cup of hot cocoa. And whenever it was possible, a Christian booklet and a text for the wall with birdies and flowers around a Bible word.

Most of the time we arranged activities in this way: At the first feast Betsie told the Christmas story of Luke 2; and then I told a Christmas story. At the second one we did the opposite—Betsie told a Christmas story and I told the Christmas story of Luke 2.

In the watchmaking business it was very busy those Christmas days. I can remember that when we went to the feast, tired after a full day, I would count for myself: "Number four. Five more evenings—and then

94

we are through Christmas!"

I knew that was wrong and I prayed: Lord, give me the miracle that I won't get tired but enjoy every Christmas feast, even if it is number ten. Should it not mean joy for everyone that You were born in Bethlehem? So Betsie and I must feel joy to be Your channel.

God answered that prayer, and all the years we did it, that miracle happened.

Now I want to tell you about a happy and a sad Christmas in my life. Christmas was a feast in our Beje home. Mother and the aunts had a gift for making it as colorful and happy as possible. I remember the holly and the mistletoe—the Christmas table with the red ribbons. Sometimes even a little Christmas tree.

Tante Jans always gave her soldiers a Christmas book and the bookstore sent us a great number from which to choose the best ones. Even as a child I remember the joy of reading through and looking at all those books.

The climax of the feast in the Beje was when we were enjoying Christmas Eve with stories and the singing of carols.

Tante Jans could tell a story so beautifully that nobody could stop listening to her. I remember that the real Christmas event was clearly

stressed by her and by Father, who read the Bible from a booklet where you could read not only Luke but also the other Gospels—Matthew 2 following Luke 2, verse 20. All the happenings then followed each other as one great story. Both Father and Tante Jans made it so clear to us that Christmas was for all of us. For me. Jesus came for me. Jesus was my friend, my Saviour.

It was Christmas, 1944. Betsie had died. I was in a hospital barracks in Ravensbruck. Dark it was in my heart, and darkness was around me.

There were Christmas trees in the street between the barracks. Why, I don't know. They were the saddest Christmas trees I ever saw in my life. I am sure it was with the purpose of blaspheming that they had thrown dead bodies of prisoners under the Christmas trees.

I tried to talk to the people around me about Christmas, but they mocked, ridiculed, and sneered at whatever I said. At last I was just quiet. It was in the middle of the night that I suddenly heard a child crying and calling, "Mommy! Come to Oelie. Oelie feels so alone." I went to her and saw a child not so young, but feebleminded.

"Oelie, Mommy cannot come, but do you know who is willing to come to you? That is Jesus."

The girl was lying on a bed next to the window, not far from my bed.

Although Oelie was completely emaciated from lack of food, she had a sweet face, beautiful eyes, and wavy hair. It was so touching to hear her call for her mother. Oelie had been operated on and the incision on her back was covered by a bandage of toilet paper.

That night I told this poor child about Jesus. How He came into the world as a little baby—how He came to save us from our sins.

"The Lord Jesus loves Oelie and has borne her punishment on the cross. Now Oelie may go to heaven, and Jesus is there right now. He's getting a little house ready for Oelie." Later I asked her what she remembered of what I had told her.

"What is the little house like?" I asked.

"It is very beautiful. There are no wicked people as in Ravensbruck—only good people and angels. And Oelie will see Jesus there."

The child added, "I will ask Jesus to make me brave when I have a pain. I will think of the pain that Jesus suffered to show Oelie the way to heaven." Then Oelie folded her hands; together we gave thanks.

Then I knew why I had to spend this Christmas in Ravensbruck—1944.

—Corrie ten Boom

The Greatest Gift

Awakening to the bright California sun streaming in my window, I realized this was my first Christmas morning as a single parent. I had been separated from my husband for less than two months and dreaded the approaching holiday season and all the emotions aroused by past remembrances.

I had been married for twenty-two years and not worked full-time in nineteen. At this point, I wasn't sure what the future held or how I would be able to help my sons with their college education. I was employed part-time at a Christian college and attending classes toward my BA at another college, but I was a long way from supporting myself. My finances looked extremely bleak.

In spite of our tight budget, God had provided some extra money so I could buy my young men some needed items such as new clothes as well as some inexpensive fun ones for their Christmas stockings.

My oldest son, Rich, was home from college for a couple of weeks. My youngest son, Mike, was on his high school Christmas break. We were enjoying quality time together before our busy schedules resumed.

Later that morning, after a breakfast of our favorite homemade

98

coffee-cake and juice, we sat around the Christmas tree, opening our presents.

"You know, Mom, even though there's less under the tree this year, somehow it seems to mean more," Rich said. "Being home for vacation with you and Mike matters a lot, too. Funny, I took all this for granted before."

"I'll be honest, guys. I've been a little apprehensive. There have been so many changes in our lives and I know the divorce has been almost as hard for both of you as it has for me." I paused, trying to put my emotions into coherent thoughts.

Mike spoke up. "I was afraid we wouldn't be a family anymore. I mean, we wouldn't feel like a family or something, but that hasn't happened."

"We are still a family," Rich added emphatically.

"Just being together is what matters," I added. "I really enjoyed having both of you here for the midnight service at church last night." With Rich living 150 miles away, we didn't get a chance to worship together very often anymore.

After most of the packages were opened, Mike handed me an envelope for my last present. I knew he hadn't been working many hours

during the school year with his studies and water polo practice, so his finances were even tighter than mine.

I held the envelope in my hand and stared at it for a moment. When I looked up, Mike's eyes met mine. "Well, open it," he said.

I did. Inside the envelope was a hand-written gift certificate which read: "Good for one oil change and a tire rotation."

Tears filled my eyes as I jumped up and hugged my youngest son. Mike's gift would save me money. However, this special present meant far more than that. Mike had given me the greatest gift he had to offer—his time, himself.

As I pondered the sacrifice my son was willing to make for me, I felt totally at peace on this special Christmas Day. I was reminded that God also made a sacrifice that first Christmas when He gave us the greatest gift He had to offer—His Son.

—Susan Titus Osborn

One More Christmas Gift

Each of our wedding anniversaries brings back a memory we cherish . . . our honeymoon trip through the Midwest in the coldest of Decembers—two days after Christmas, in fact. The roads were snow-packed and slick. Originally concerned that we might lose our hotel reservation because of our slow-going, we began to fear we might not make our honeymoon suite at all.

Suddenly we noticed lights coming up behind us. As Bill saw it was a truck, he slowed to let it pass. Raised in snow country, we'd learned the value of traveling behind a trucker—low wind resistance, lights to follow, a trail "blazed." But most of all, we valued the safety of traveling alongside a driver who practiced it every day.

As the trucker neared, he must have noticed JUST MARRIED smeared all over our car because as he passed by slowly, the guys in the cab grinned and waved. Suddenly they rolled down their window and pushed out two trumpets which they began playing—*Here Comes the Bride.* The truck's side wore the name of a band, which explained everything.

101

We rolled down our window and listened as they passed. Within moments we watched their tail lights get smaller and smaller as we couldn't safely keep up with them. We began to feel fearful again, when suddenly, the tail lights got bigger and bigger.

They stayed with us for the next 60 miles until we took the off-ramp into our honeymoon city. We honked our thanks to them and whispered our thanks to Him, for what we knew to be one more Christmas miracle.

—Mary Bahr Fritts

Jesus' Birthday Party

Have a party in honor of Him whose birth we celebrate. Include in the celebration an older person who would otherwise be alone, someone you have just met, a young person away from home, and one or two very special friends such as a pastor or teacher who is important to your family's life.

Some special things to make or do might include:

Birthday-card place cards.

A special star-shaped cake with white and yellow icing full of fruit, to represent the fulfillment of the seed of promise.

A table centerpiece of a basket or small wooden box of clean straw surrounded by small packages made to represent gold, frankincense and myrrh. Someone might tell about the three gifts and what they might have represented or how they might have been used.

Example

Gold was the most precious metal symbol of God's most precious gift. Perhaps this provided the financial means for the trip

Mary, Joseph, and Jesus made to Egypt and for their stay there when they were forced to hide from Herod.

Frankincense and myrrh were important spices used in Jewish rituals as incense and as burial spices. Perhaps these gifts hinted at the fulfillment of the Old Law as well as the crucifixion of Jesus that was to come. Someone has suggested that Mary may have kept these precious spices and used them to embalm the body of our Lord thirty-three years after his birth.

—Gloria Gaither and Shirley Dobson

White Linen And Pink Ribbons

Growing up in Missouri during the depression years, times were hard and money was scarce. The farms in the southeast had turned to dust bowls. We could no longer depend on the land for a living. It became a custom to celebrate Jesus' Birthday with Christmas at our church.

I looked forward to this special Christmas of 1932. I was praying for a beautiful baby doll I had picked from the big mail order catalog.

"Look, Mamma, isn't she beautiful?" I shouted.

"Oh, Honey, don't wish too hard. Money is pretty hard to make now days, with no work in sight." She smiled sadly as she handed the catalog back to me.

What's money got to do with my doll? I wondered. True, the price in the catalog was marked sixty-nine cents, but Santa Claus would bring me my baby doll. I prayed and knew I would get my doll.

A month before Christmas, I watched Mamma sew a complete layette. I believed it was for a new baby in our church family.

Mamma was smiling and hummed a favorite hymn as her nimble

105

fingers lovingly held the fragile white linen and pink ribbons. She sewed for weeks. As soon as breakfast was finished she hurried through the morning chores, anxious to start sewing again.

"Why are you so happy, Mamma?" I asked.

"Daddy got a job, Honey. Now will you try to sit still while I finish this sewing?"

"Yes Mamma, I'll try." I watched her laying each finished piece side by side on her soft feather bed. A little white dress trimmed around the neck and hem with pink ribbons. Next, a tiny white slip with Irish lace around the bottom. Fluffy white bloomers was next to be finished with a tiny pink ribbon bow tacked to the outside of each leg. The last garment, and I'm sure the most difficult, was a beautiful bonnet with its wide brim starched stiff. It was also trimmed in white lace with pink ribbons laced through with plenty left over for the tie underneath the baby's chin.

She placed the precious garments between thin tissue paper and stored them in her dressing table drawer.

One day they were gone.

"Mamma, did you give the little clothes to the new baby?" I asked.

"What baby, Honey?" she asked, smiling a sweet secret smile.

On Christmas Eve we all gathered at our church. I was nestled

106

between Mamma and Daddy in our pew. I felt very secure as daddy smiled down at me.

"Excited, Hon?" he asked.

"Yes." I could hardly whisper, I was so nervous. I had seen several dolls hidden in the branches of the big green Christmas tree; but mine wasn't there.

Chubby Mrs. Snider was huffing and puffing the music out of the old pump organ, as Carols were being sung.

Suddenly, the entry door of the church was flung open and a loud voice boomed, "HO! HO! HO!" Santa Claus had arrived!

I hid my head under Daddy's arm, so excited and a little scared of Santa. I peeked as he came down the aisle, next to our pew. He was chubby, wearing a red suit trimmed in black with white fur on his red hat. He turned his smiling face toward us and gave me a jolly wink, as he passed by. I couldn't take my eyes off him. I watched him call the names of all my friends. To my horror, all the dolls had been handed out.

Tears filled my eyes. Had my prayer been unheard? Had Santa missed me.

Then I watched as he reached behind the glistening tree and he held

107

a doll. "Virginia Edwards, come up here and see what Santa has for you," his voice boomed.

I shot out of the pew and ran as fast as my eight-year-old legs could run. I held my breath and reached out my arms as Santa lay the beautiful doll in my arms. I couldn't move. I stared at Santa so stunned I couldn't even look at my doll.

Santa spoke, putting his arm around my shoulders, "There you go little lady, back to your seat." He gave me a little nudge and I walked slowly, as if in a dream, back to our pew. I slipped between Mamma and Daddy as I looked up and they were smiling down at me. I could see tears of love on each face.

Like any real new mother, I unwrapped the white blanket from my baby doll. My eyes opened wide as I looked in awe at my baby dressed in white linen and pink ribbons.

"I love you, Mamma," I whispered. I thanked God for my answered prayer.

—Virginia A. Moody

Real Christmas Joy

Those new clothes I've been waiting for
      I finally get to buy!
And I'm in such a festive mood,
      For Christmastime is nigh.

The store is crowded while I shop
      But I don't mind a bit—
Arms full, I rush to try things on,
      Wondering how they'll fit.

While walking past the twinkling lights
      Hanging in the window,
Something there draws my attention
      And my steps begin to slow . . .

A little boy is pressed to the glass,
      His eyes shining and bright—
My glance falls to his ragged coat
      And tears I have to fight.

109

He points to toys he cannot have
　　His lips are moving fast;
His mom looks sad as she takes his hand
　　And tries to pull him past . . .

All the things she cannot afford
　　But wishes that she could-
Her little boy deserves much more;
　　He's always been so good.

The clothes I hold now seem heavy;
　　They weigh upon my arm-
And suddenly my shopping spree
　　Has lost all of its charm.

Laying aside the things I chose,
　　I hurry out the door-
Knowing Jesus wants me to
　　Be generous to the poor.

I slip my gift into her hand
　　And feel my spirit soar . . .
For her eyes glisten as she leads
　　Her son into the store.

—Denise A. DeWald

110

A Brother Like That

A friend of mine named Paul received a new car from his brother as a pre-Christmas present. On Christmas Eve, when Paul came out of his office, a street urchin was walking around the shiny new car, admiring it. "Is this your car, Mister?" he asked.

Paul nodded, "My brother gave it to me for Christmas."

The boy looked astounded. "You mean your brother gave it to you, and it didn't cost you nothing? Gosh, I wish . . . "

He hesitated, and Paul knew what he was going to wish. He was going to wish he had a brother like that. But what the lad said jarred Paul all the way down to his heels. "I wish," the boy went on, "that I could be a brother like that."

Paul looked at the boy in astonishment, then impulsively he added, "Would you like to ride in my car?"

"Oh, yes, I'd love that!"

After a short ride the urchin turned, and with his eyes aglow said, "Mister, would you mind driving in front of my house?"

Paul smiled a little. He thought he knew what the lad wanted.

111

He wanted to show his neighbors that he could ride home in a big car. But Paul was wrong again.

"Will you stop right where those two steps are?" the boy asked.

He ran up the steps. Soon Paul heard him coming back, but he was not coming fast. He was carrying his little crippled brother. He sat down on the bottom step, then sort of squeezed up against the lame child and pointed to the car.

"There she is, Buddy, just like I told you upstairs. His brother gave it to him for Christmas, and it didn't cost him a cent, and some-day I'm gonna give you one just like it; then you can see for yourself all the pretty things in the Christmas windows that I've been trying to tell you about."

Paul got out of the car. "Why don't we start seeing them right now," he said and lifted the little lad on to the front seat of his car. The shining-eyed-older brother climbed in beside him and the three of them began a memorable holiday ride.

That Christmas Eve Paul learned what Jesus meant when He said, "It is more blessed to give . . . ."

—C. Roy Angell

112

Shopping Cart Caroler

I headed for the door, anxious to get my last-minute Christmas shopping done. I was looking forward to completing this long and complicated process of choosing and buying . . . by myself!

"Mommy," began my four-year-old daughter, Kelsey. "I want to go, too."

"Okay," I said reluctantly, "But let's hurry."

In the car on the way to the department store we rehearsed the Christmas carols she would be singing the next day. Kelsey, along with a preschool choir, would be performing for a group of "grandma's and grandpa's" at a local retirement home.

Approaching the main entrance of the store I realized that a couple hundred other shoppers had the same idea, this cold December evening. Trapped in the crowd, we were herded through the doors and over to the waiting shopping carts.

I hoisted Kelsey up into the front of the cart and noticed her outfit. She wore a pink play dress with red tights and tennis shoes. Her hair needed a brisk combing and her face revealed traces of red and

green Christmas cookies. Maybe I shouldn't have let her come, I thought. Oh, well. No time to worry about her appearance now. I shoved the cart into the flow of traffic, hoping I wouldn't see anyone I knew.

At first I tried to hustle through the aisles, but the store was so packed that I slowed to a comfortable cruise. This was definitely going to take longer than I expected.

Sitting happily in the basket, Kelsey once again began her repertoire of Christmas songs. Focused on finding that perfect gift at a reasonable price, I didn't notice the effect her singing had on the shoppers around us.

I looked up in time to see a grin on an older man's face. Then, with Kelsey's voice blaring *Deck the Halls* at full volume, we passed a younger man with a cart load of stereo equipment. He looked at Kelsey and said, "That's great!"

A red-haired woman stopped next to us with eyes full of amusement. She listened to Kelsey's entire rendition of *Away in the Manger.* As Kelsey moved into the second stanza of *Oh, Christmas Tree,* I pushed the cart to the front of the store. I jostled for position

114

in the check out line, and a man leaned over and said, "That's caroling at its best."

At the checkout counter I gazed up and down the long line of waiting customers and saw all of their eyes focused on my daughter. I noticed their tense, pre-Christmas "hurriedness" seem to relax and soft smiles crease their faces.

Then I glanced down at my little singer. At that moment she was not the most attractive performer, but she was beautiful to me. Suddenly I was very glad I'd brought her. This sneaker-clad caroler had reminded me and the other harassed shoppers that this season represents so much more than hurried shopping.

—Michelle R. Wilson

A Simpler Gift

A growing list of Christmas gifts has clouded up my mind . . .
For the next few weeks, free time will be a rarity to find!

Christmas bags and packages are stacking up galore . . .
And yet my shopping list reveals I need to purchase more!

At home our tree remains undone, the lights are who knows where.
Ornaments lay in a box . . . the star still packed with care.

Holiday cookies . . . I've yet to bake, no Keebler elves around,
To mix and shape, bake and ice the culinary mounds!

Christmas cards I need to write, notes I'd like to send . . .
I frantically race to and fro . . . it seems to never end!

Jingle bells and Santa Claus, stockings still to fill . . .
Tylenol I'll need on hand to face the charge card bill!

I hope this season passes soon . . . the fun's too much for me!
Gifts and treats and Santa Claus and lovely ornate trees.

It seems something's been overlooked that simply cannot be!
I've made a list and checked it twice or have I failed to see

116

The subtle hints around me that imply there's something more . . .
a feeling that a calm exists somewhere amidst the roar.

Things that tell of a simpler gift, not made to adorn a shelf,
A gift to embrace within the heart, the gift of Christ Himself.

No media hype or party invites, no wrappings of glitter or gold,
No royalty sent to welcome the King . . . even though His birth
was foretold.

Livestock and hay, a manger so meek, guests that were dusty and worn,
A babe clothed in rags, amidst the feed bags, The King of all
Kings was born!

How oft I tend to lose amidst the clamor of the world,
The quiet call to draw unto this humble King, our Lord.

Oh may our hearts draw near this year to Christ, the King of Kings . . .
The reason for the season and for whom all heaven sings!

So come ye faithful and draw near for Christ was sent to all,
One silent night, one holy night, in a humble manger stall.

—Patty Stump

117

The Story Behind
I Heard the Bells on Christmas Day

During a Christmas cantata last year, I listened to the words of this piercing song for the first time, *I Heard the Bells on Christmas Day*. The cynical tone in the third verse amazed me.

Why so bleak for such a joyous season?

Henry Wadsworth Longfellow's journals tell the story. In 1863, when the poet penned the poem, originally called Christmas Bells, peace on earth was only a dream. The Civil War had torn most every American family with horror and despair.

Longfellow's family was not an exception. The day the poet heard the Christmas bells, he also received the heart-wrenching news that his son, a lieutenant in the Army of the Potomac, had been seriously wounded in battle. As the bells chimed "peace on earth, peace on earth," his son was dying, the result of man's hate. Longfellow struggled with the conflicting messages.

"There is not peace on earth," he wrote. "Hate is strong/And mocks the song/Of peace on earth/Good will to men."

But the bells kept ringing and ringing. It was as if God, who also lost a Son to man's vengeance, said: Hate is strong, but I am stronger. Rest in Me, Peace will come.

—Melissa Wilson

118

Through Children's Eyes: "Christmas"

Born in Bethlehem.
Cast of angels and kings,
shepherds and lambs,
a Christmas Star,
and Presents.
Hot cocoa on cold winter nights,
stockings on fireplace
above smoking logs.
Scent of pine from Christmas Tree.
Mom hanging lights,
hilarity!
Avoidance of mistletoe, and
tones of Perry Como.
Okay then Bing!
Bikes Dolls Skates.
Gold Frankincense Myrrh.
Presents.
Joseph, with Mary atop a tired donkey

119

travel toward their destiny.
Human Holiness born in humble stable.
Shepherds saw angels,
heard singing went seeking.
Wisemen followed His Star.
"No Room in the Inn" for Jesus, they claimed.
"He can have my room," says a child,
and fill it
with His Presence.
   —Jeri Chrysong and sons, Luc and Sam Alexander

120

An Unforgettable Gift

On Christmas morning, 1912, in Paducah, Kentucky, fourteen-year-old Charlie Flowers and his three brothers and two sisters huddled in their beds, fully-dressed, trying to keep warm as the wind howled outside their small frame house.

It was a desperate time for the family. Earlier that year their father had died. The coal had run out. There was little money—none for gifts. Their tree with decorations made from scraps of colored paper had been given to them the night before by a local merchant who said he "could not sell this last one."

To pass the time, the children joked and shouted stories to one another across the hallway. Then suddenly a noise from the alley at the rear of the house broke into their games.

"Charlie," his mother called, "would you see what's going on out there?"

Charlie pulled on his shoes and ran out back. There stood a man with a wagon. He was bent over a load of coal, shoveling it into the shed as fast as he could.

"Hey mister, we didn't order any coal," Charlie shouted. "You're

121

delivering it to the wrong house."

"Your name's Flowers, isn't it?" the man asked, still shoveling.

Charlie nodded.

"Well then, there's no mistake. I've been asked to deliver this to your family on Christmas morning." Then he turned and looked the awe-struck boy square in the eye. "And I'm under strict orders not to tell who sent it," he teased.

Charlie Flowers died last spring at age 96. And right up to the last year of his life, not a Christmas went by that he didn't tell the story of that sub-zero Christmas morning of his boyhood when two men gave his family an unforgettable gift.

It wasn't the coal that was remembered or cherished, Charlie often said—welcome as it was—but rather what two men brought to his needy family. The one, for his gift of recognizing a great need and taking the time to do something about it. And the other man, being willing to give up part of his own Christmas morning to deliver it.

That gift of so long ago has continued to warm the Flowers family from one generation to another, as Charlie's son—my husband—calls to mind these two unknown men each Christmas morning and whispers a prayer of thanks.

122

And since we have become Christians, our thanks as a family has deepened. For now we see the powerful parallel between this story of long ago and the profound story of nearly two thousand years ago when the Father Himself recognized our great need and did something about it—by sending His son Jesus into our midst—the most unforgettable gift of all.

—Karen O'Connor

"Look, I Found God!"

The children were helping decorate the house for Christmas. As they set up the nativity set, they discovered the baby Jesus was missing. Imagine a nativity set with no baby Jesus!

Suddenly, two-year-old Clinton popped up from behind the davenport, holding high the missing Babe and excitedly called, "Look. I found God!"

May we all be able to say the same!

—Venus E. Bardanouve

123

Snowballs

1/2 cup dried apricots
1/2 cup raisins
1/2 cup unsweetened pitted dates
1 1/2 cups Rice Krispies
1/2 cup pecans or walnuts, finely chopped
1/2 teaspoon vanilla
1/2 teaspoon fresh orange peel, grated juice from one orange
1/2 cup flaked coconut

In a blender or food processor grind the apricots, raisins, and dates until smooth. Add the Rice Krispies, nuts, vanilla, orange peel, and orange juice. Shape into 1-inch balls and roll in flaked coconut. Do not bake. Store in airtight container in refrigerator. Makes 36 Snowballs (two equal one serving).
77 calories and 1.3 fat grams/two

124

The Real Christmas

I remember one Christmas Eve when I met a photographer from one of the metropolitan newspapers. Bard's regular assignment was riding the night cruiser his newspaper used to follow police calls.

Bard and his reporter "specialize in chasing down catastrophe and sudden death. We're supposed to be a hard-boiled crew. But even to us, Christmas is a nightmare . . . double the drinking, shoplifting, accidents, calls for disturbing the peace . . . or at least it was a nightmare until one night about a week ago."

At 9:30 p.m., over their police radio came an All Units in the Vicinity call: "A missing juvenile, boy, age 11. Last seen wearing a blue flannel shirt and blue jeans."

"We were cruising in the Hollywood area where the boy was last seen," the photographer said, "but who's going to spot one eleven-year-old in jeans in that rush of night shoppers?"

At 10:15 p.m. Bard and his reporter stopped in at Hollywood police station to make a routine check and there was the missing juvenile in a thin flannel shirt and beat-up jeans brought in by a burly patrolman. Under his arm he clutched a package. He was as

125

close to tears as a tough eleven-year-old could be. It was an old story, the one the desk sergeant had written down. A working mother, no father, a tough kid running loose, the mother panicky—only this one had a new twist.

"No, I won't let you see what's in my package," the boy was protesting violently. "But I'll tell you what's in it. It's a necklace and earrings." The sergeant's eyebrows shot up and his lips tightened grimly. The boy couldn't help noticing and he blurted out, "My mom saw 'em last Easter, but she couldn't afford 'em, see? I been payin' on 'em for eight months. Today I walked all the way to the boulevard 'cause I needed the carfare for the last payment. I was almost home when he"—he shot a baleful look at the patrolman—"hauls me down here. I ain't done nothin'. And if you tell my mom . . ." he was fighting those tears again " . . . it's a Christmas surprise, see?"

The photographer cleared his throat while he was telling me this part of his story. "So maybe we're a hard-boiled bunch. And suspicious. Wouldn't you be? He was a tough little kid. But I knew darn well nobody was gonna tell—if his story checked."

It checked. The jeweler remembered the boy well. "Been coming into my place with nickels and dimes and quarters every month since last April," he told the desk sergeant.

126

"Well," said the photographer, "we all felt pretty good. I mean really good. Like after you've said a prayer or something. One of the prowl cars took the kid on home . . . he'd walked from way down in the south end of town . . . and the rest of us stood around that bare police station and did something I don't ever remember doing before. Even if it was only December 17 we all wished each other a Merry Christmas . . . us, newspapermen and policemen . . . the guys who thought Christmas was a nightmare! Imagine that crazy little kid—buying his mom a Christmas present, at Easter!"

—Pat Boone

127

While Shepherds Washed
Their Socks By Night

I knew it wouldn't be the usual Christmas when the children started singing, "While shepherds washed their socks by night."

I could identify with those shepherds and their laundry. Our clothes hamper was constantly choking on pint-size, black-and-neon holiday sweatshirts that proclaimed—presumably to the bearer of gifts—"I've been good."

The sweatshirts came from a summer clearance sale. "When can we start wearing our new sweatshirts?" my two children begged. Never mind that it was ninety-five degrees outdoors.

"Not until Thanksgiving," I ordered. "Let's not rush the season."

The question came up again when store shelves began touting holiday cards for early birds. "Not until after October." I had weakened.

They donned those sweatshirts at 6:43 a.m. the first of November. The holiday had begun.

"When are we getting our tree, Mom?" came the chorus.

"A week before Christmas," I said firmly. The tree, of course, arrived four weeks before Christmas. The children decorated the tree

128

up to a height of four feet. Then it was on to "Deck the Halls."

The crèche took its honored place on the fireplace hearth. My eight-year-old (the organizer) posed all the animals on one side and all the shepherds and kings on the other.

I knew something was "Awry in the Manger" when the six-year-old (the free spirit) decided her Barbie doll needed to pay the crèche a social call. She rolled Barbie up to the scene in a pink plastic Corvette.

"I've been good," the eight-year-old announced hopefully as he tacked his stocking to the fireplace. His concern was understandable since I hadn't put any presents under the tree yet. I knew what would happen when I brought the presents out of hiding. The organizer rearranged the gifts so that his were on one side of the tree and his sister's on the other.

"I've got seven and you've got eight," he muttered. "No fair." It wasn't *Joy to the World* I heard them singing to each other.

On Christmas Eve, I tucked the twosome in bed at eight and started the laundry—those sweatshirts were dirty again. At ten, I checked in on them. There's something about sleeping children that reminds me of angels. *O Holy Night,* I hummed to myself. "O Come, O Come, Immanuel," I prayed. "You've been good to us."

—Jeanne Zornes

129

'Twas the Night Before Jesus Came

'Twas the night before Jesus came and all through the house
Not a creature was praying, not one in the house.
Their Bibles were lain on the shelf without care
In hopes that Jesus would not come there.

The children were dressing to crawl into bed
Not once ever kneeling or bowing their head.
And Mom in her rocker with baby on her lap
Was watching the Late Show while I took a nap.

When out of the east there arose such a clatter
I sprang to my feet to see what was the matter.
Away to the window I flew like a flash,
Tore open the shutters and threw up the sash!

When what to my wondering eyes should appear
But angels proclaiming that Jesus was here.
With a light like the sun sending forth a bright ray
I knew in a moment that this must be THE DAY!

The light of His face made me cover my head-
It was Jesus . . . returning just like He had said.
And though I possessed worldly wisdom and wealth,
I cried when I saw Him in spite of myself.

In the Book of Life which He held in His hand
Was written the name of every saved man.
He spoke not a word as He searched for my name;
When He said, "It's not here," my head hung in shame.

131

The people whose names had been written with love
He gathered to take to His Father above.
With those who were ready He rose without a sound
While all the rest were left standing around.

I fell to my knees, but it was too late:
I had waited too long and thus sealed my fate.
I stood and I cried as they rose out of sight:
Oh, if only I had been ready tonight.

In the words of this poem the meaning is clear:
The coming of Jesus is drawing near.
There's only one life and when comes the last call
We'll find that the Bible was true after all!
　　　　　　　　　　　　　　　　　—Unknown

132

Just Like Grandpa's

From time to time our grandchildren stay overnight or spend a weekend with us. One Sunday morning, when Cody was eight years old, we were almost ready to leave for church when Cody noticed his grandpa's necktie. "Grandpa, do you have a tie I can wear today?"

"My ties are too big for you, Cody. Maybe Grandma can find one that your daddy or your uncle David wore when they were boys."

My search for a tie was unsuccessful. So Cody's obvious disappointment prompted me to ask, "Would you like to have us give you a necktie for Christmas?"

At that he brightened and said, "I'd like that, Grandma, because I really want one—a blue one, just like Grandpa's."

Although I was unable to find one like Grandpa's, I did find a blue tie that was even prettier.

On Christmas morning—after giving both of us a kiss and a big bear hug—Cody hurried over to the tree and stood there for a long time looking at all the packages underneath it.

Shortly after that I went into the kitchen, and Cody quickly

133

followed me. "Grandma," he said, his eyes bright with excitement as he looked up at me, "Is there a tie in one of those presents under the tree?"

Smiling, I admitted, "There might be one in there, Cody. Do you think there is?"

"Yes, 'cause I told you I really want one."

Cody was confident that we would give him a necktie for Christmas, for we had promised to do so. Remorsefully, I remember times when I have let my requests be made known to God only to fret and worry instead of waiting in childlike anticipation for Him to grant them.

—Marjorie K. Evans

134

A Journey to Christmas

It happened to us practically every year. Christmas Day seemed to sneak up on my wife, Susan, and me. We may have had our presents ready, our house decorated, our Christmas meal planned, but our hearts were distracted and unprepared. The day passed in a flurry of busyness, hugs, gifts, feasts. By early evening we collapsed while the kids played with their new toys. Wearily we promised ourselves and God: "Next year it will be different!"

The answer to our problem is found in the past. Our ancestors called it "Advent," which means "Coming." It describes the period which begins four Sundays before Christmas Day. It is the liturgical season of Christmas.

Like so many other people, Susan and I forgot that Christmas is a season and not merely a day. We counted the shopping days, but overlooked the calendar of the Early Church.

As soon as we began to celebrate the season of Advent, December became a journey. A journey toward the day of Christmas. A Journey toward a stable and an impossible birth.

The wise men were prepared for a journey toward a stable. They

135

had gifts to offer. They were ready to worship, and that is precisely what they did.

This December, Susan and I will take a journey, embarking on the first Sunday in the month. We will depart from the busyness of the world and proceed, by God's grace, toward a quiet, simple, lowly place: the stable where the King of the universe will be born once again into our hearts. As we follow the star, we will have time to prepare for the scene that we will witness at our journey's end. Along the way we hope to find a gift to offer along with the gifts of frankincense, gold and myrrh from the wise men.

I am certain that our gift will be the gift that Jesus desires most: the gift of ourselves, discovered during our journey toward Christmas.

—Michael Card

Make a "Jesse Tree" This Christmas

This year, by starting early, you can add something new and special to your Christmas celebration: a Jesse Tree.

You've never heard of a Jesse Tree? It's a pre-Christmas tree that is becoming more popular both in churches and homes. It is a "tree" that can be made by your whole family, your youth group, or even by you.

The name comes from Isaiah 11:10 where Christ is said to be "a root of Jesse." The Jesse Tree is a bare, dead tree (or a very large branch). It can be put up anytime after Advent begins, and is decorated, not with lights, but with ornaments made in shapes that symbolize Old Testament characters. These symbols recall the people who lived before Christ, but who, through their place in history, helped lay the way for Him.

The Jesse Tree is not meant to take the place of your Christmas tree. It is to be a prelude, as the Old Testament is to the New. So the Jesse Tree is replaced by the living, green Christmas tree that symbolizes the eternal life Christ brought. The Christmas tree is lighted to show that the Light of the World has come in the form of a Baby.

137

Your decorations for the Jesse Tree can be made from any material you want—metal, baked flour and salt dough, or wood. Paper ones are the most popular because they can be made even by your little brothers and sisters. You can use colored construction paper or paint and crayons on white paper. The decorations can be as elaborate as your artistic skill, or they can be simply outlines.

Use the puzzle below to determine what symbol represents each Old Testament character, then make them for your Jesse Tree, adding others you think of. Your Christmas season guests can play the game, too, by trying to identify each character by his or her symbol on the tree.

Character		**Symbol**
1_____	Adam and Eve	a. ladder
2_____	Noah	b. temple
3_____	Joseph	c. crown
4_____	Jacob	d. harp
5_____	Ruth	e. scissors
6_____	Moses	f. golden calf
7_____	David	g. sun
8_____	Daniel	h. apple
9_____	Solomon	i. altar
10____	Jonah	j. blades of wheat
11____	Aaron	k. coat of many colors
12____	Joshua	l. ark
13____	Samson	m. lion
14____	Abraham	n. whale
15____	Esther	o. stone tablets

Puzzle answers:
1-h; 2-1; 3-k; 4-a; 5-j; 6-o; 7-d; 8-m; 9-b;
10-n; 11-f; 12-g;13-e; 14-i; 15-c

—Betty Steele Everett

139

"Mommy, Is Jesus Excited About His Birthday?"

"Mommy, is Jesus excited about His birthday?"

My four-year-old's question took me by surprise. I looked up from my giftwrapping to reply, "I suppose He is, Daniel. You get excited about your birthdays, don't you?" My answer satisfied the deep preschool curiosity. However, my answer did nothing to satisfy me.

My mind wandered back to Daniel's first birthday. Obviously beyond his memory, it was clearly etched in mine. We had just moved from a small apartment into our very first house. Months of packing, cleaning, and repairing had left us simultaneously weary and thrilled to make the move.

Daniel's first birthday was to be the first remotely large gathering we had ever hosted. On that day I consulted my carefully-prepared list and began to work. Floors were scrubbed and dishes washed. The cakes were baked and frosted to perfection. Serving pieces were located and removed from yet unpacked boxes.

My husband arrived home from work in time to shower and change before the guests began to arrive. Everything in place, we were ready for

140

the party. The doorbell rang; the first guest entered; and Daniel began to scream!

Suddenly, I realized what had happened. Following me around all day, my little toddler had received only a minimum of attention. As the day wore on I attributed his increasing agitation to excitement. Now I understood. He was simply frightened. He didn't understand my frantic preparations. All he knew was that his normally-attentive mommy was behaving very strangely. Now, with guests arriving, he was afraid of what might happen next.

Daniel finally did calm down and enjoyed the remainder of his party. I came to a valuable realization. I hadn't planned the party for him at all. I had planned it for everyone else. I had taken what should have been a wonderful day and filled it with preparations and hoopla that meant nothing to him.

"Mommy, is Jesus excited about His birthday?" The words echoed in my mind. I had never really thought about it before. Were all of the plans and preparations I was undertaking really going to please Him? Or, like Daniel's first birthday, was I planning the celebration to please everyone except the "Guest of Honor?"

What does Jesus want for His birthday? Perhaps it is simply the love, faithfulness, and devotion He always desires from us.

—Susan Waterman Voss

141

Tea Leaf Christmas

One snowy, icy and blustery day just before Christmas, my friend, Debe, and I decided to treat ourselves to a special day of antiquating. We each had the holiday blues. My Christmas was not the same since Mom's death. I especially missed her as my best friend.

Memories of garage sales and various antique stores filled my mind. During spring and summer Mom and I used to go antiquating on Saturday mornings. We traveled the suburbs and surrounding towns. Each antique shop was quaint and dilapidated. The paint on the buildings was peeling. Rusted farm tools surrounded some stores, but inside were treasures. The more junk, the better we liked it.

We concentrated on items Mom collected. She always wanted to add to her Tea Leaf Ironstone collection of pottery. Tea Leaf was made in England around 1900. The pottery was simple but elegant, bluish white with a copper leaf design and a band of copper lustre. Mom had about thirty pieces —good pieces were hard to find.

After our treasure hunt we would stop for ice cream. Those were times when I learned something about the past as Mom told me about her childhood on a farm in Lancaster, Missouri. She was raised during

142

the depression. I can remember her telling me that the Lancaster town cafe used Tea Leaf dishes on their tables.

The copper inlay on the Tea Leaf reminded Mom of her mother's copper kettle where applesauce was stirred over the fire. When Mom died, I inherited her collection of Tea Leaf.

As Debe and I approached the store that day in December, I ran ahead. The door creaked as we opened it. Inside we could smell hot apple cider and freshly-brewed coffee. Dusty relics of the past filled the store. Dried apples in cans, wreaths, and candies lined the shelves. It made me feel like I was back at my grandparent's farm.

In the book section, a title startled me: Grandma's Tea Leaf Ironstone. The first thing I saw on the cover of the book was a teapot. It looked familiar.

Suddenly, I remembered that I owned a teapot similar to the one pictured. Something nudged me to buy the costly book. Uncertain of my purpose, I stood at the cash register and counted out the dollars.

Sleep did not come easily that night. I tossed and turned for hours. My eyes watched the lighted numbers on my digital clock slowly change from midnight to two o'clock. The only way to sleep was to solve the mystery of why the book's cover seemed so familiar

to me. I got out of bed and turned on the light. The book was on the nightstand. I stared at the picture on the book jacket. The teapot's size and shape were identical to mine. The copper leafing stood out. Surely there was a hidden meaning. I felt like my childhood detective heroine, Nancy Drew.

Something stirred my memory. I rummaged in my billfold and found an almost forgotten, coffee-stained business card with the name "Annise Doring Heaivilin, Author-Collector, $20.00 paid on Tea Leaf creamer and sugar 6/1/79."

That's what this is all about! I mused. I remembered a specific shopping adventure with my mother where she bought a pitcher at an antique store in Riverside, MO. The owner of the shop, a heavy-set gray-haired woman, told mom she was writing a book. She asked for written permission from Mom to photograph the teapot. She gave Mom the business card receipt.

Could this possibly be the same book? Thumbing through the book I found Mother's name, Mrs. J.B. McClure, in the acknowledgment page in the front of the book.

The picture on the cover was my teapot! My feelings boiled like a cup of freshly brewed tea.

144

Now I knew why I had to have that book. It was my special Christmas present from the past. Though Mom was gone, her love was forever intertwined with mine through the teapot we had purchased together so long ago. Over the years and through the snow, in a dusty antique shop I had found a book which linked me with my Mother and gave me peace for the holiday.

—Mary Linn McClure

Immanuel—God With Us

Christmas, again. Another waiting queue; my patience almost gone. Even in a Christian bookstore, I felt I might lose control as the "seasonal help" wasn't quite up to speed. When did Christmas become synonymous with buying and waiting? I inwardly griped. Little did the three kings know the treacherous trend of gift-giving they were establishing on that first Christmas so many years ago.

I had to look away. Yes, the sales person was nice and helpful, smiling at each new customer, but for the moment she wasn't smiling at, or helping, me.

To distract myself from potentially lethal impatience I looked through the store's seasonally-decorated windows. I caught sight of two Asian toddlers prancing like puppies in their excitement. They had thick, shiny black hair cut across their foreheads into a healthy sets of "bangs." Their little faces filled with the Christmas wonder (which my grumbling face lacked) bore the classic perfection of porcelain dolls. The vivacious skipping and dancing stopped abruptly as they caught sight of the baby Jesus and the nativity scene on display in the window.

146

Behind their invisible leashes, the toddlers' pretty young mother finally caught up with her wiggly toddlers. Looking in need of a break herself she brought the children into the store, knelt down, and began, in reverence, to tell, with the aid of the nativity figurines, the Christmas story to her children. I watched the threesome, enchanted.

The mother spoke a different language, but the story was the same. I recognized the pantomime of tired and pregnant Mary as she sat upon the donkey's back with Joseph as her guide. I understood each "No Room," "No Room," "No Room," and corresponding negative bobbing of this young mother's head. I too was blinded by Heaven's brightest star, envisioning flying angels proclaiming baby Jesus' birth and, along with the wide-eyed toddlers, I "heard" the baby's first cry while stiff-legged stable animals looked on.

The narration over, the mother rose to leave. Her gaze on me told me I'd been caught eavesdropping. I smiled apologetically for the invasion. She returned my smile, conveying that she somehow knew she was telling the Christmas story for my benefit as well as for her children.

In that moment, perhaps for the first time, the realization of the

147

universal appeal of Jesus Christ hit me; the "good tidings" for all people, not just English-speaking Americans. He is Immanuel—God with us. He is everyone's God.

An impatient poke from behind told me to "snap to and pay attention" as it was now my turn and my pensive state was holding up the line.

"Next, ma'am," repeated the counter girl, smiling, finally, at me.

My spirit rejuvenated, I handed over my purchases, silently thanking God for the gift my Asian sister had given me.

—Jeri Chrysong

148

Beyond The Manger

Hear the lowing of the cattle,
smell the wonder in the air.
See the hands of Joseph folded
as he kneels in silent prayer.
Does he see beyond the manger?
Does he see a king that day?
Does he recognize this baby . . .
as the one to show the way?

Hear the music from the Heavens
smell the perfume in the air.
See the hands of man uplifted
as God gives Himself to share.
Even though some have not met Him
He came for all of us today.
From a manger in a stable . . .
He has come to show the way.

—Marcia Krugh Leaser

149

I Could Have Been A $10,000 Winner

My ultimate Christmas episode happened when I was five years old and videos didn't exist (at least not for the general public). If they had, I would have won the $10,000 prize on America's Funniest Home Videos. The electricity of excitement filled the pine-scented air. The church was decked with boughs of holly and filled to capacity as moms, dads, grandparents, aunts and uncles flocked to see their little cherubs perform.

Our time finally came and my Sunday School class lined up on stage. Our teacher, Miss Millie, instructed us to stay right beside the rail that outlined the stage. All went smoothly as we recited memory verses and sang carols; that is until it happened. Being a nervous five-year-old, I had been wriggling around during the performance. When we finished and the class turned to leave, I couldn't move. All my little friends passed by and I stood there alone. It wasn't stage fright. Somehow, I had wedged my knee between the rail slats. Snickering rippled through the audience and within seconds turned into a wave of laughter. Not only was I stuck, frightened and humiliated,

I couldn't even yell out for someone to call 911. Like video cameras, 911 didn't exist.

I frantically looked out into the audience and found my parents. My eyes met my Father's eyes. That's all it took. Dad jumped up (with a grin on his face, I might add) and came to my rescue. I knew he could save me. With tear-filled eyes as I concentrated on Dad, my humiliation and fear diminished and the crowd became a shadow. It took several minutes of twisting and more intentional wriggling to get me free, but the laughter faded and the rest of the play went on without a hitch.

That night turned into a good teaching tool. Dad taught me not only to look to him when I found myself stuck—unable to move with nowhere to turn—in this pageant of life. He also taught me to look into my Heavenly Father's eyes of love.

—Georgia Curtis Ling

151

Reflections of an Innkeeper

Scene: A hill outside Jerusalem, in the spring of 30 AD. An old man is praying. He turns and speaks:

"You might wonder why I'm standing out here on this hillside praying when there's so much excitement here in Jerusalem this Passover season. Let me tell you a little about my life story, and then maybe you'll understand.

"My name is Solomon. I was named for David's son, Israel's greatest king. I've achieved my parents' goals for me: great wealth. I started as a stable boy, and worked my way up in the innkeeping business until I became manager of the Bethlehem Inn. Under my leadership, the inn prospered, achieving the highest honor in our industry when we were designated the only "Star-Rated" facility in Bethlehem.

"Shortly after we earned that designation, I made a mistake that has haunted me ever since—until today. It was a little over thirty years ago. Emperor Caesar Augustus had called for a census. What a windfall for the innkeepers of Bethlehem! Every Jew in Palestine who traced his ancestry to David came to Bethlehem to register. The streets were swarming and I had raised all my rates to the maximum.

152

"But there was a rumor that some kind of royal visitor would make an appearance. While I was never a religious man, I did remember the words of the prophet Micah, who wrote of Bethlehem, "But thou, Bethlehem of Ephrathah, though thou be little among the thousands of Judah, yet out of thee shall he come forth unto me that is to be ruler in Israel . . . " Just imagine—a King coming to our city!

"Well, if a King was coming to our city, what better place for him to stay than at the "Star-Rated" Bethlehem Inn? We set aside our finest room, furnishing it with the best appointments. We called it "The Royal Berth."

"Once all the other rooms were filled, I instructed the staff to turn away anyone else. But then one of my staff came to me with a very touching story. There was a young man and his fiancee who desperately needed a place to stay. 'Could we make an exception? The young woman is pregnant and her time is obviously very near.'

"But what was I to do? The King still might come. The thought of the prestige of having my inn chosen by a King, not to mention the added revenue, far outweighed any pity I might have had. I did feel sorry for them, though, so I told them they could sleep in the stable with the animals.

"Then some really strange things began to happen. In the middle of

153

the night I heard a baby's cry and knew she'd given birth. Without baby furniture, she laid the little boy in one of the animal feeding troughs. Then I became aware of a really bright light. I could hear music with many voices—like a great choir. Later a group of shepherds came and said the music was angels singing, 'Glory to God in the highest, and on earth, peace among men of goodwill.'

"Days later, three kings came to Bethlehem. They said that they had been following a star from the east, and that it had not only led them to Bethlehem, but to my very Inn. They asked where they might find the one who was 'born King of the Jews.' What was I to answer them? The only newborn around was that little baby. I told them about him— but a king? They went down there to look, and I was amazed when those men actually worshipped that little baby and offered him rich gifts. Imagine!

"And then I began to wonder—could it be that, because of my own greed and ambition, the King I had been waiting for had been born in my stable when there was a lovely room standing vacant? As time passed, I became more convinced of it. I was devastated and cried out to God for forgiveness, but it seemed the heavens were brass. I was doomed to carry this burden of guilt to my grave.

"Until today, thirty-three years later. Did you hear about the young rabbi who caused such a stir earlier today? The crowds went wild, and kept calling him the 'King of the Jews' and 'The Son of David.' He's about thirty-three. Could he be that baby who is grown up? I had to find out and pushed my way through the crowd to the front row, in time to see him pass by. As he did, his eyes caught mine. And I knew. It was Him! It seemed like he physically touched me. I cried out in my heart, 'Forgive me, O Lord my King—I didn't know what I was doing.'

"And then, it was as if I heard him reply, 'Because you believe in me, all your sins are forgiven.' And I knew. I was forgiven! Incredible!

"And so, just now, I felt I had to come out here to thank God for lifting my burden of guilt. Now I know we did have a King in our Inn that evening so long ago—but He didn't stay in the Royal Berth."

—Richard J. Lindholtz

155

Mary's Song

Blue homespun and the bend of my breast
keep warm this small hot naked star
fallen to my arms. (Rest . . .
you who have had so far to come.) Now nearness satisfies
the body of God sweetly. Quiet he lies
whose vigor hurled
a universe. He sleeps
whose eyelids have not closed before.
His breath (so light it seems no breath at all) once ruffled
the dark deeps to sprout a world.
Charmed by dove's voices, the whisper of straw,
he dreams,
hearing no music from his other spheres.
Breath, mouth, ears, eyes
he is curtailed
who overflowed all skies,
all years.

156

Older than eternity, now he
is new. Now native to earth as I am, nailed
to my poor planet, caught that I might be free,
blind in my womb to know my darkness ended,
brought to this birth
for me to be new-born,
and for him to see me mended
I must see him torn.

—Luci Shaw

Stay By My Cradle

Christmas is my time of year! I love everything about it. I actually like the hassle, the gift buying, the baking, the caroling, and the decorating. Nothing should spoil the celebration of our Savior's birth. But I do remember one Christmas when a near disaster gave me my own personal Christmas miracle and demonstration of God's love.

That particular Christmas Eve found me as a young mother of two energetic boys. Ty was a rambunctious three-year-old, while Christopher (my Christmastime baby) would be two in a few days. I was especially looking forward to this holiday because both boys were old enough to understand the excitement and really participate in the celebration. I would get to see Christmas through the eyes of a child again.

All of the preparations had been made. The boys had hung their stockings and set up the tiny manger scene which awaited the figure of the baby Jesus. Finally, worn out, they were carried off to bed by their daddy and were soon fast asleep.

We, however, were left to assemble toys and help Santa fill the stockings. It was midnight before we too could prepare for bed. I checked on the boys who were sleeping peacefully in their room.

158

Above Christopher's crib hung an old, framed Sunday School poster I had received when I was a child. It depicted the nativity scene with Mary and Joseph gazing at their new baby with all the animals attending. I had always loved that picture, and it hung in the nursery all year round.

As my husband finished getting ready for bed, I decided to wind down by reading the Christmas story. All of a sudden, the loudest noise that I had ever heard exploded through the house! I sat up with a start realizing that smoke was pouring into our bedroom from the hall. But it wasn't smoke; it was dust—plaster dust! I bolted into my little boys' room and tried to peer through the choking cloud. As things began to settle, I saw a large hole had been torn through the corner of their room. Broken studs, insulation, and bricks were scattered everywhere.

My eyes finally focused on Ty, sitting up in his bed rubbing his sleepy little eyes. I looked toward Christopher's crib. It was a pile of broken slats looking like huge pick 'em up sticks.

Where's Christopher? I wanted to scream. The mattress was awry; plaster board and rubble everywhere. But where is Christopher? An image of a broken and torn little body being ripped from his crib flashed into my mind.

159

Just then a confused little head poked up from under the debris and mattress. Oh God, thank you. It's Christopher! I ran to him and scooped him up out of the pile. As I did, my eyes were instantly, magnetically drawn to the nativity picture which still hung on the wall above. A quiet voice within my heart said, "Your baby is fine, mother. I protected him." I knew then, without even looking, that Christopher was not injured.

In a few hours it was Christmas. I never opened the nursery door that day. We had no time to dwell on the destroyed room or the possible tragedy that might have occurred. In our house, no midnight nightmare would spoil Christmas for us because a baby born long ago was still looking down and protecting us.

—Joan K. Weaver

160

A Box of Blessings

Our 7-year-old daughter exclaims, "Mommy, it's time to open another present!" No, it's not Christmas morning, but it is time to help keep our family's thoughts focused on the true meaning of Christmas. The children can hardly wait to dive into our "Box of Blessings," a special box which holds 24 gifts for the Advent season.

The first present introduces the idea. On December 1, I open the large gift-wrapped box containing 24 attractive gifts, and read the enclosed tag to the family: "Today we are beginning a Christmas project. We will open a different present for the next 24 days to help remind us of God's most precious gift "His Son Jesus."

To make your own "Box of Blessings," simply wrap a large box with Christmas paper, wrapping the lid separate. Gather 24 visual aids, wrap them, write out tags for each (object lesson, Scriptures and discussion questions), and place the gifts in the box. Here are some suggestions.

* Several pieces of any kind of food. READ: Does food always stay the same even after a long time? No, it changes when it gets old, doesn't it? But Jesus never changes; He is always the same.

161

(Hebrews 13:8) Why do you think it is important that Jesus never changes?

  * A heart-shaped object. READ: Hearts remind us of love. We love others, but did you know that God loves us even more? (Corinthians 13: 4-7) How many things about love can we find in these verses?

  * A piece of soap. READ: Jesus washed His disciples' feet to show them that they should be servants to each other. (John 13:5) How can we be a servant to each other?

  * A piece of flat bread for each person. READ: Jesus was tempted just like we are. (Matthew 4:1-11) When we are tempted, how can we resist the Tempter like Jesus did?

  * A rubberband. READ: See this rubberband? When we pull and stretch it, it becomes tight. That's a good example of how we feel inside when we worry. If we don't stretch it, the rubberband is soft and relaxed. (Philippians 4: 6-7) God wants us to relax in Him. If we are uptight, what do we need to do so that we can relax inside?

  * A blank piece of paper with isn't erased off. READ: When you make a mistake in writing, you can erase it and start over again. When you do something wrong, called sin, you can ask Jesus to for-

162

give you and He will forget all about it. You can start over again. (Ephesians 4:32) What is something each of us did wrong lately that Jesus has forgiven us for?

* A match. READ: The deeds we do are either valuable or worthless. (1 Corinthians 3:12,13) What deeds are each of us doing that will be considered good in heaven? What deeds will be judged worthless and burned up?

* A happy face sticker. READ: Is there something you can do to make God happy? (Colossians 3:20) What are some ways each of us can be obedient today?

* A tiny globe or picture of the earth. READ: God made the earth and everything in it. That includes each of us. (Genesis 1:1; Psalm 139:13-16) Do you know that you are special and important to God?

*(This one is perfect for the last gift): A photograph of each child when they were a baby. READ: You used to be a baby, didn't you? So was Jesus. Just as you are growing up, Jesus grew up so that He could one day become our Savior. (Luke 2:1-20) What do you want to be when you grow up? In what way can each of us continue to have the Christmas spirit every day of the year?

—Kathy Collard Miller

163

Annie Lee's Gift

Mrs. Stone's second-grade was not itself today. One glance across the room proved Christmas had begun its countdown. At this time of the year Mrs. Stone admitted to only partial control of her students. It was amazing how such a lovely holiday could turn her well-disciplined students into spirited elves—with horns.

"Teacher?" A child's voice called from the activity table. Stepping over scraps of paper decorating the carpet, Mrs. Stone moved to where a few children were making calendars for their parents' Christmas gifts.

"Yes, Annie Lee." returned Mrs. Stone.

The little girl tossed back her long, shining hair and answered politely. "Uh . . . if I finish my calendar, could I take it home tonight? My mother wants to see it. She might have to go in the hospi . . . "

"No, Annie Lee," responded Mrs. Stone automatically. "You may take it home on Friday like everybody else."

Annie Lee started to protest but the teacher moved quickly from the table, brushing silver glitter from her skirt. To the rest of the class Mrs. Stone announced, "All right boys and girls, it's time to clean up."

164

"Ahhh . . . ." The expected groans of disappointment came and went.

Seated at her desk, Mrs. Stone opened the lid to a small wooden chest. The tune of *Silent Night* was immediately recognized by the children. They listened quietly.

"Shay, would you begin our show-and-tell today?" Mrs. Stone asked while closing the music box.

The boy came to the front of the room and said with a slight boast, "I'm getting a red bike for Christmas."

Mrs. Stone closed her eyes in exasperation.

Annie Lee's turn to share was next. Her long hair reflected the sunshine coming through the window as she came forward.

"My mother is sick and can't make the cookies for our party on Friday," she announced.

Mrs. Stone's eyes flew open. I can't believe Mrs. Brown is using that same excuse, thought Mrs. Stone. She couldn't attend P.T.A. or parent-teacher conference for the same reason. Some parents try to get out of their responsibilities.

Annie Lee edged close to the teacher's desk and the music box. Her eyes sparkled as she spoke and one finger tenderly touched the wood. "When my mother gets well, she's going to buy me a music box like yours, Mrs. Stone."

"That's nice, Annie Lee, but it couldn't be exactly like mine. You see, this is very old. It was my great grandmother's music box. Some day, I'll give it to one of my children."

The following day Annie Lee brought a thin strip of red velvet ribbon up to the teacher's desk.

"Mother went to the hospital last night but she gave me this ribbon to wrap around the gift I made for her," she said.

"The ribbon is very pretty," said Mrs. Stone. "I'm sorry your mother is in the hospital."

Annie Lee began again with her request. "Daddy said I could bring the calendar to the hospital if you—"

Mrs. Stone interrupted. "I've already told you that we will wrap them tomorrow and take them home on Friday."

Annie Lee looked disappointed and then suddenly brightened. "Mother made this for you!" she said happily and laid a red velvet bookmark in front of Mrs. Stone. She turned and skipped away. The sheen was missing from Annie Lee's hair today; it was dull and tangled and uncombed.

Friday came. The children filled their chairs—but Annie Lee's chair was empty. Uneasiness moved Mrs. Stone to sit down. One

166

more burden added to twenty-five years of accumulated frustrations was more than she could bear. A student monitor entered the room and handed Mrs. Stone a folded note. Trembling, she read the principal's hastily written note. "I thought you'd want to know. Annie Lee Brown's mother died early this morning."

Somehow Mrs. Stone managed to get through the day. When the party was over and the children had gone home to enjoy their holiday, Mrs. Stone stood alone in her classroom and cried. She cried for Annie Lee, for Annie Lee's mother, and for herself. She cried for the gifts, the calendar that was intended to bring joy but didn't, and the red velvet bookmark—so undeserved.

It was very late at night when Mrs. Stone left the school. She carried the music box in her hands as if it were a Wise man's treasure itself. Stars twinkled above to light the way to Annie Lee's house. Mrs. Stone looked up to the brightest star and prayed the music box would help return Christmas to both their hearts.

—Glenda Smithers

167

Hospitality to the Children in Your Life

When school lets out for the holidays, it's time to make memories and have some fun in the kitchen, playroom or den. Here are some good ideas for keeping youngsters entertained during the Christmas season by involving them in the holiday festivities.

Kids' Cooking Party

A kids' cooking party is an excellent way to show hospitality to the children in your life (including yours, those of close friends, grandchildren, or a few of the youngsters on your block). You can invite an assortment of kids to come over for an afternoon of cooking, tasting and decorating gingerbread boys and girls (which you have already made or bought) using raisins, colored icing, red hots (tiny spicy cinnamon candy) or M&Ms. They can take home some of the cookies to share.

Or if you're really brave and jolly, you can have each guest don an apron and cook up a storm! You should have all the ingredients ready to make one gigantic pizza or a bunch of individual pizza pies.

168

Your youthful guests can decorate a giant chocolate chip cookie or make a "Star of Bethlehem." Your junior cooks can also create special Christmas treats for the birds.

Santa Apples

Every year in the Neeley home, "Santa apples" (for looking, not eating) are made the way their grandmother used to prepare them years ago. Here are the necessary ingredients:
- 1 upside-down apple (shined with Crisco) for Santa's body
- 3 or 4 cranberries on toothpicks for his legs and arms (allow the arms to angle in a slight "V" and the legs to come a bit forward)
- 1 toothpick to be used in the back as a prop to help the pudgy old elf stand up
- 1 large marshmallow for the head
- cranberries for his red hat
- several fresh cloves for his eyes and mouth and the buttons down the front of his coat
- a ball of cotton attached with glue (and coming to a point) for a beard

Holiday Cones

We used to make these for birthday parties, but they are delicious and fun to make and eat at Christmas. You will need:

- 1 regular-sized box of cake mix (your favorite flavor) and any ingredients the mix requires
- 24 flat-bottomed ice cream cones
- frosting (and sprinkles, if desired for decoration)

Directions: Prepare the cake mix by following the instructions on the box. Spoon cake batter into each cone until it is half full, and then place the cones on a baking sheet or in a muffin tin. Bake for 30 minutes at 350 degrees. Cool before frosting. Sprinkle red or green sugar crystals on the top. You can decorate them to look like Frosty the Snowman or Santa.

Frosty: Use white frosting and white coconut for his body, black licorice for his hat, and red candies for his eyes and mouth.

Santa: Spread frosting on top of the cupcakes. Then add coconut for a beard and the fur of the hat (mini-marshmallows can also be used for white), chocolate chips or raisins for eyes, and red hots (cinnamon candies) for a mouth and hat.

—Cheri Fuller

Fresh Fruit Pie

Makes 8 servings

1 1/2 cups unsweetened flaked coconut
2 egg whites, lightly beaten
1 can (20 ounces) unsweetened crushed pineapple with juice
1 tablespoon cornstarch
2 bananas, sliced in orange juice and drained
1 pint fresh strawberries, sliced (or kiwi or papaya)
unsweetened flaked coconut to garnish
additional strawberries to garnish

Preheat oven to 325 degrees. Toss coconut and egg whites together and press into a pie pan. Bake for 10 minutes; cool. (Add more coconut and another egg white if you want the mixture to create a pie shell.) In a saucepan, mix the pineapple and cornstarch and cook over medium heat until thickened. Layer the bananas, strawberries, and pineapple; and sprinkle with coconut and strawberries to garnish. Or pour pineapple over crust, and arrange the bananas and strawberries over the top. Chill for 3 hours.

—Pamela Smith, R.D.

171

Home for Christmas?

I remember the last year my siblings and I gathered our broods together and piled into our parents' home for Christmas. We were a Norman Rockwell painting come to life—three generations gathered in nostalgic reunion. To the casual viewer, the pictures we took show Christmas the way it should be celebrated. Everyone was home for the holidays.

But pictures can be deceiving. Even as we smiled into the camera, my siblings and I knew we would never again be together in this way. Our mother was dying. At 31, I was not prepared to lose a mother.

Earlier in the year, my mother had discovered she had cancer of the colon. Operation followed operation, and gradually the doctor's optimistic prognosis turned to resigned pessimism. As the holidays approached, it became clear that "home for Christmas" would not be what I had anticipated. We had planned for a celebration, but now we had to say good-bye.

By Christmastime, Mother could stay up for only short periods of time. During one of her sitting-up periods, we went next door to her brother's home. Our pictures showed her curled up in a chair, watching

the little ones roast marshmallows in the fireplace. She spoke of recovery. She believed she was going to get better. She was going to beat the monster that had invaded her body. We encouraged her in her hope, but we all knew she was dying.

One evening, with great effort Mother left her bed and dressed in her finest. For thirty minutes we gathered in various poses before her piano for family pictures. It was the last time she sat up. Six weeks later we finished the roll of film by taking pictures of her flower-banked grave.

No one—especially a mother—is supposed to die at Christmastime. In our minds, Christmas is forever-linked with family togetherness. If anything mars the holiday reunion . . . well, Christmas isn't Christmas.

The Christmas of my mother's dying prompted me to examine my concept of what the celebration is all about. I recognized what lay at the heart of my holiday discontent: a distorted image of Christmas as the ultimate family reunion.

Sometimes we sense an emptiness even when the whole family is home for Christmas. Behind the smiling faces lurk problems undetected by the camera: an illness, a financial crisis, an estranged child, old conflicts never healed. Having convinced ourselves that family togetherness

173

is synonymous with Christmas, we refuse to make room for problems.

Yet, I ask myself, isn't that what the first Christmas was all about? That birth in Bethlehem was hardly a subject for a Norman Rockwell painting. Something was terribly wrong with God's family, and He sent His Son to fix it.

Separation formed an essential part of God's plan for Christmas. And death was not too far behind.

I wonder how the Father must have felt as He looked down from Heaven? The celebration took place on earth. Heaven must have been very lonely.

Spending Christmas with family will always be my first choice. I continue to seize every opportunity to celebrate this day with our scattered offspring. But when we are separated, Christmas will still be Christmas.

The celebration is not about earthly reunions. It is about a Son who left home 2,000 years ago that one day God's children might all experience the ultimate family reunion.

—Joy P. Gage

Who Cared About a Jewish Baby Born in Bethlehem!

If Dan Rather had been living in 1809, his evening news broadcasts would have concentrated on Austria . . . not Britain or America.

The attention of the entire world was on Napoleon as he swept across helpless hamlets like fire across a Kansas wheat field. Nothing else was half as significant on the international scene. The broad brush strokes on the historian's canvas give singular emphasis to the bloody scenes of tyranny created by the diminutive dictator of France. From Trafalgar to Waterloo, his name was a synonym for superiority.

At that time of invasions and battles, babies were being born in Britain and America. But who was interested in babies and bottles, cradles and cribs while history was being made? What could possibly be more important in 1809 than the fall of Austria? Who cared about English-speaking infants that year when Europe was in the limelight?

Somebody should have. A veritable host of thinkers and statesmen drew their first breath in 1809:

- William Gladstone was born in Liverpool.
- Alfred Tennyson began his life in Lincolnshire.
- Oliver Wendell Holmes cried out in Cambridge, Massachusetts.
- Edgar Allan Poe, a few miles away in Boston, started his brief and tragic life.
- A physician named Darwin and his wife called their infant son Charles Robert.
- Robert Charles Winthrop wore his first diapers.
- A rugged log cabin in Hardin County, Kentucky, owned by an illiterate wandering laborer was filled with the infant screams of a newborn boy named Abraham Lincoln.

All that (and more) happened in 1809 . . . but who cared? The destiny of the world was being shaped on battlefields in Austria—or was it? No, indeed!

Only a handful of history buffs today could name even one Austrian campaign—but who can measure the impact of those other lives? What appeared to be super-significant to the world has proven to be no more exciting than a Sunday afternoon yawn. What seemed to be totally insignificant was, in fact, the genesis of an era.

176

Go back eighteen centuries before that. Who could have cared about the birth of a baby while the world was watching Rome in all her splendor? Bounded on the west by the Atlantic . . . on the east by the Euphrates . . . on the north by the Rhine and Danube . . . on the south by the Sahara Desert, the Roman Empire was as vast as it was vicious. Political intrigue, racial tension, increased immorality, and enormous military might occupied everyone's attention and conversation. Palestine existed under the crush of Rome's heavy boot. All eyes were on Augustus, the cynical caesar who demanded a census so as to determine a measurement to enlarge taxes. At that time who was interested in a couple making an eighty-mile trip south from Nazareth? What could possibly be more important than Caesar's decisions in Rome? Who cared about a Jewish baby born in Bethlehem?

God did. Without realizing it, mighty Augustus was only an errand boy for the fulfillment of Micah's prediction . . . a pawn in the hand of Jehovah . . . a piece of lint on the pages of prophecy. While Rome was busy making history, God arrived. He pitched His fleshly tent in silence on straw . . . in a stable . . . under a star. The world didn't even notice. Reeling from the wake of Alexander the Great . . . Herold the Great . . . Augustus the Great, the world overlooked Mary's little Lamb.

It still does.

—Charles R. Swindoll

No Vacancy

The sign warned: SNOW AHEAD CHAINS REQUIRED. My husband Lewis said, "Janet, look for the next exit sign. Cars are skidding off the road and we need to put on our tire chains." Within ten miles, the snow blew so hard that it was almost impossible to see the highway markers on the freeway. We couldn't believe it. Never had we expected weather like this en route to San Diego, California from Phoenix, Arizona.

Lewis slowed to below ten miles an hour. At last I glimpsed an exit sign and we skidded precariously on the packed snow on the off ramp. Through the darkness we saw the Christmas lights of a convenience store and Lewis pulled in. It was only eight days until Christmas. We hadn't expected to be making this trip now, but Lewis' sister had called that her husband was critically ill in the hospital—could we come? As I had packed, I muttered, "What terrible timing!" But, of course, we had to go.

Lewis buttoned his jacket and found the tire chains and flashlight in the trunk. He instructed me, "Janet, you'll have to move the car forward when I tell you—just inches—till I can hook the chain together."

178

I nodded. I needed to keep the car window open to hear Lewis' instructions and snow and cold blew in taking my breath away. Poor Lewis down under the car.

Over and over again Lewis tried to connect the chains but couldn't get them to meet. Should we spend the night in Banning? But the NO VACANCY sign at the nearby motel told me the answer. But we also couldn't proceed without chains.

Suddenly the face of a black man with a knit cap pulled down over his ears appeared outside my car window. I was already shaking with cold yet a new shiver of fear made me tremble. Lewis heard voices and stood up.

"Can I help you?" the stranger asked.

"I'm trying to get chains on my car. They don't fit."

"Maybe I can help. Let's see."

I could hear the men talking as I continued to follow their instructions driving forward and backward. They mentioned letting some air out of the tires so the chains would fit. It seemed that the tires on this car were larger than on our last car and the chains were made to fit a smaller size.

It was several hours later that the second tire was completed. Lewis'

179

jacket was soaked and he shivered with cold.

"Let me go into the store and see if they have hot coffee to warm us up," I offered.

Lewis answered, "Sounds wonderful."

I grabbed my purse and started toward the lights.

Suddenly I slipped on the ice and fell. I lay there looking up at the sky with swirling whirlwinds of snow over me. What else could happen?

I struggled to my feet and returned with coffee for all of us several minutes later. Lewis' hands shook as he thanked the stranger for his time and energy.

"The Lord sent you to us tonight," I added as I looked into his friendly face and eyebrows flecked with heavy snowflakes.

"I believe in the Lord, too. By the way, I have a room at the motel. There's no vacancy but you may have my bed. I'll sleep on the floor."

At that moment, I knew what Mary must have felt when she and Joseph found a place to stay so many Christmases ago.

Lewis shook hands and said, "Thank you my friend, for your generous offer, but since we have the chains on now, we must push on. My brother-in-law is dying."

Earlier, I had briefly thought God's timing was terrible—but God had shown me how He provided what we needed when we needed it.

—Janet Lowe

Finding Christmas

"Mom, I called to tell you I won't make it home for Christmas this year."

Shock numbed my heart! This would be the first Christmas in 35 years that our family would be separated. Our daughter, pregnant and due to deliver on December 29th, was planning a quiet day at home with her husband. And now our son, calling from the other coast, was telling us his recent promotion with the airlines wouldn't permit free time during the busy holiday season.

At our house, Christmas was important. We lived for Christmas. I shopped for gifts throughout the year. Baking began after Thanksgiving with pies, cookies, and breads and ended with hand-dipped chocolates. On Christmas Eve, the celebrations started with a buffet and the opening of one gift. Christmas morning, we opened the remaining gifts and ate a family breakfast. Later in the day, we celebrated again, dining on turkey and playing board games, which were often accompanied by much laughter and raucous bickering about cheating.

181

Later that week, my husband Bob and I gloomily discussed the options of a tree, decorations, cookies, pies, turkey, buffet, and gifts. We decided that this year, we would forgo all the trappings of the holidays and eat dinner out.

Bob suddenly looked old. Occasionally he sighed and then stared into space. As the weeks passed, I found myself devoid of my usual holiday spirit. Depressed, I felt as though I had lost someone dear. After all, we are told that Christmas isn't Christmas without family. But this year, we would have no one. No one. We had lost Christmas!

One day in early December our daughter called. "So Mom, what are you doing? Have you got the freezer filled with goodies yet?"

Sadly, I told her our plans. "What did you and Dad do for the holidays before we were born?" she asked.

It was then I remembered those early years—newly married, with no money, and living two thousand miles from family. Suddenly, I was excited. Why couldn't we have a merry day without our children? After all, we could call them. I could still make candy and cookies and mail them off—a touch of home for them. I knew this holiday season would be more difficult for them than it was for us. My selfish thoughts dispersed as I rummaged in the closet for the cookie tins.

Bob dug out the Christmas lights and outlined the house with color. Soon, the fragrance of cinnamon and nutmeg filled our home. We surrounded the créche with pine boughs from the fir tree in our garden.

Christmas Eve arrived, and Bob and I ate our buffet. We opened one gift, sat before the fire, and listened to Bing Crosby Christmas albums.

At Midnight Mass, the young priest stood before an altar resplendent in red poinsettias and pine boughs, and his words touched my heart. "Do not be afraid, for behold, I bring you good news of great joy which shall be to all the people . . . ."

On Christmas morning we opened gifts and prepared the turkey. At dusk, peace surrounded us as we walked hand-in-hand across the lawn and watched as stars began to glow. Colorful lights brightened the neighborhood. A soft breeze hummed through the fir trees. Smoke from the neighbors' fireplace blanketed the air with the smell of comfort.

We hadn't lost Christmas after all. It had always been there, waiting for us in that silent, holy night.

—Lois Erisey Poole

183

Granny's Jam Cake

4 cups flour
2 cups sugar
2 cups blackberry jam (seedless)
3 sticks of butter
6 eggs
2 teaspoons soda
3 tablespoons buttermilk
2 teaspoons cloves
2 teaspoons nutmeg
2 teaspoons cinnamon
1/2 cup chopped nuts

Sift together flour, sugar and spices. Mix soda, buttermilk, jam and beaten egg.

Combine all ingredients. Add nuts last. Butter a 9 inch tube pan (or two loaf pans); line with waxed paper. Turn batter into pans and bake at 325 degrees for one hour and fifteen minutes or until cake leaves side of pan.

Turn out of pan and frost with Caramel Frosting.

184

Caramel Frosting

3/4 cup butter
1 1/2 cups brown sugar
1/4 cup pus 2 tablespoon milk
3 cups powdered sugar
1 teaspoon vanilla

Melt butter and add brown sugar. Add milk and bring to a boil. Remove from stove and let cool. Add powdered sugar and vanilla. Beat until creamy and smooth.

—Georgia Curtis Ling and "Granny" Pearl Curtis

185

"We've Been Waiting for You, Mother"

We were new Christians and our family devotions were rather sporadic, but at Christmas we had Advent Devotions, with all the pomp and circumstance of the holiday season: Christmas carols, candles and a crèche.

Each evening during Advent, the four weeks before Christmas, the children took turns adding a piece to the clay crèche we had made, anticipating the coming of Christmas Eve when they could place the Christ Child in the manger.

My husband was attending college three nights a week and I was trying to be "Super Mom," adding to the strain of an already-busy household.

The "busyness" of the season was intoxicating. The warm, sweet smell of endless dozens of Christmas cookies filled the house. I was "Christmasing" the house with tinsel garlands, greens, bows, and poinsettias and sewing special Christmas garments for my children, besides the regular busy schedule of wife and mother of two toddlers and a ten-year-old daughter. Weariness draped itself like a weight on my shoulders.

186

That particular evening I tidied the boy's bedroom and got them ready for bed. I put their toys in the closet, then went into the kitchen to finish the dishes.

When I had finished, I returned to the boys' bedroom to gather them for evening devotions. My eyes couldn't fathom the sight they beheld. The room looked as though a cyclone had hit it. Toys were everywhere. Every toy they owned was on the floor, and if it came apart the pieces were scattered.

That was the straw that broke the camel's back. I exploded! I spanked both boys, all the while yelling at them for creating the mess. I couldn't cope. My weariness had crowded out any patience, understanding, or humor.

I ran to my bedroom, slammed the door shut, threw myself on the bed and sobbed. I was so ashamed.

I lay there crying for quite some time. Finally, gathering my composure, I wiped my tear-stained eyes and sheepishly walked into the living room to apologize to my beloved children.

It was dark except for the three candles on the Advent wreath. The candleglow illuminated my three children sitting on the couch: my daughter, her brothers on each side, and an open Bible on her lap.

187

"We've been waiting for you, Mother."

I rushed to hug them as I apologized and professed my love for them through choking tears of joy. What a blessing I had in these precious children, and what a lesson I learned about love and acceptance from them.

—Ina Gesell

188

Credits

Priceless Gift from *Decision* magazine, Billy Graham Evangelistic Association, December, 1993.

Giving in Secret from *Creating Christmas Memories*, Cheri Fuller, Honor Books, Oklahoma, 1991.

Silent Night from *Follow the Year*, Mala Powers, HarperCollins Publishers, Inc., New York, 1985.

Christmas Card Activities from *Let's Make a Memory*, Gloria Gaither & Shirley Dobson, Word Inc., Texas, 1983.

The Gift of Eternity from *Decision* Magazine, Billy Graham Evangelistic Association December, 1993.

Gabriel's Questions from *When God Whispers Your Name*, Max Lucado, Word, Inc., Texas, 1994.

Seasonal Seesaw (adapted) from *Normal Is Just A Setting On Your Dryer*, Patsy Clairmont, Focus on the Family, Colorado, 1993.

A Cup of Christmas from *If Teacups Could Talk*, Emilie Barnes, Harvest House Publishers, Eugene, Oregon, 1994.

Corrie's Christmas Memories from *Corrie's Christmas Memories*, Corrie ten Boom, Fleming H. Revell, a division of Baker Book House Company, Michigan, 1976.

The Greatest Gift from *Rest Stops for Single Mothers*, Susan Titus Osborn and Lucille Moses, Broadman & Holman Publishers, Tennessee, 1995.

Jesus' Birthday Party from *Let's Make a Memory*, Gloria Gaither & Shirley Dobson, Word Inc., Texas, 1983.

A Brother Like That from *Baskets of Silver*, C. Roy Angell, Broadman Press, Tennessee, 1955, Renewed 1983.

Twas the Night Before Jesus Came, Bethany Farms, Carrollton, Illinois, 1994.

A Journey to Christmas from *Decision* magazine, Billy Graham Evangelistic Association, December, 1995.

Mary's Song from *Polishing the Petoskey Stone*, Luci Shaw, Harold Shaw Publishers, Illinois, 1990.

Hospitality to the Children in Your Life from *Creating Christmas Memories*, Cheri Fuller, Honor Books, Oklahoma, 1991.

Fresh Fruit Pie from *Eat Well, Live Well*, Pamela Smith, R.D., Creation House, Florida, 1992.

Who Cared About a Jewish Baby Born In Bethlehem from *Growing Strong in the Seasons of Life*, Charles R. Swindoll, Zondervan, Michigan, 1983.

*All of the above have been *Used by permission of the publisher or author.*

Contributors

Venus E. Bardanouve— PO Box 367, Harlem, MT 59526. (406) 353-2397.

Martha Baker—12601 Hinson Road, Little Rock, AR 72212. (501) 224-7171.

Jeri Chrysong—19022 Hamden Lane, Huntington Beach, CA 92646.

Joan Clayton— PO Box 606, Portales, NM 88130.

Denise A. DeWald—1744 Swenson Road, Au Gres, MI 48703. (517) 876-8718.

Roberta Donovan— 711 Virginia Street, Lewistown, MT 59457.

Tamera Easterday— PO Box 887, Tehachapi, CA 93581. (805) 822-6927.

Marjorie K. Evans— 4162 Fireside Circle, Irvine, CA 92714. (714) 551-5296.

Mary Bahr Fritts— 807 Hercules Place, Colorado Springs, CO 80906.

Joy P. Gage— 2370 S. Rio Verde Dr., Cottonwood, AZ 86326.

Ina Gesell—1201 W. Valencia #212, Fullerton, CA 92833. (714) 680-6240.

Anita Heistand— Rt. 2, Box 484, Galena, KS 66739. (316)856-5157.

Betty Huff—10025 El Camino, #25, Atascadero, CA 93422. (805) 461-5619.

Veda Boyd Jones— 505 W 34th Street, Joplin, MI 64804.

Helen Hertha Kesinger— 221 Brookside Drive, Paola, KS 66071-1111. (913) 294-2937.

Mary Lou Klingler— 300 North Drive, Paulding, OH 45879-1025. (419) 399-3089.

Marcia Krugh Leaser— 2613 C. R. 118, Fremont, OH 43420. (419) 992-4307.

Deborah M. Lewis— PO Box 2029, Lake Arrowhead, CA 92352. (909) 337-1506.

Jami C. Lewis— PO Box 1854, Chino Valley, AZ 86323. (520) 636-2943.

Georgia Curtis Ling — 4716 W. Glenhaven Drive, Everett, WA 98203. (206) 259-9136.

Lynette S. McBride— 684 Fairway Lane, Gunnison, CO 81230. (970) 641-4238.

Mary Linn McClure— 5205 N.W. 84th Place, Kansas City, MO 64154. (816) 741-0083.

Kathy Collard Miller and D. Larry Miller— PO Box 1058, Placentia, CA 92871. (714) 993-2654.

Virginia A. Moody—17402 114th Pl., NE, Granite Falls, WA 98252-9667.

Karen O'Connor— 2050 Pacific Beach Drive, #205, San Diego, CA 92109. (619) 483-3184.

Susan Titus Osborn— 3133 Puente Street, Fullerton, CA 92835. (714) 990-1532.

Luis Palau— Luis Palau Evangelistic Assoc., PO Box 1173, Portland, OR 97207-1173. (503) 614-1500.

Lois Erisey Poole— PO Box 3402, Quartz Hill, CA 93586-0402.

Laura Sabin Riley— 10592 Del Vista Dr., Yuma, AZ 85367. (520) 342-7324.

Karen Robertson— 33140 Claremont Street, Wildomar, CA 92595. (909) 678-3030.

Christi Anne Sheppeard— 700 E. Washington #230, Colton, CA 92324.

Patty Stump— PO Box 5003, Glendale, AZ 85312. (602) 938-1460.

June L. Varnum— PO Box 236, Loyalton, CA 96118. (916) 993-0223.

Susan Waterman Voss— Box 136, Atkins, IA 52206. (319) 446-7402.

Joan K. Weaver— RR 2 Box 52, Lewis, KS 67552. (316) 659-3253 or 659-3363.

Michelle R.Wilson— 1127 Ginger Avenue, Eugene, OR 97404-1586. (541) 688-7619.

Jeanne Zornes—1025 Meeks St., Wenatchee, WA 98801.

Other Books by Starburst Publishers

(Partial listing— full list available on request)

God's Vitamin "C" for the Christmas Spirit   —Kathy Collard Miller & D. Larry Miller

Subtitled: *"Tug-at-the-Heart" Traditions and Inspirations to Warm the Heart*. Written in the same spirit as best-selling *God's Vitamin "C" for the Spirit*, this collection will rekindle new and old traditions for celebrating the Christmas season. This keepsake includes a variety of heart-tugging thoughts, stories, poetry, recipes, songs and crafts. Christian writers and speakers, such as Pat Boone, Cheri Fuller, Gloria Gaither, Joni Eareckson, and Michael Card combine their talents to produce a book that is sure to encourage a time of peace, relaxation, and the building of your own cherished Christmas memories.

(hardcover) ISBN 0914984853   **$14.95**

God's Vitamin "C" for the Spirit   —Kathy Collard Miller & D. Larry Miller

Subtitled: *"Tug-at-the-Heart" Stories to Fortify and Enrich Your Life*. Includes inspiring stories and anecdotes that emphasize Christian ideals and values by Barbara Johnson, Billy Graham, Nancy L. Dorner, Dave Dravecky, Patsy Clairmont, Charles Swindoll, H. Norman Wright, Adell Harvey, Max Lucado, James Dobson, Jack Hayford and many other well-known Christian speakers and writers. Topics include: Love, Family Life, Faith and Trust, Prayer, Marriage, Relationships, Grief, Spiritual Life, Perseverance, Christian Living, and God's Guidance.

(trade paper) ISBN 0914984837   **$12.95**

God's Chewable Vitamin "C" for the Spirit

Subtitled: *A Dose of God's Wisdom One Bite at a Time*. A collection of inspirational Quotes and Scriptures by many of your favorite Christian speakers and writers. It will motivate your life and inspire your spirit. You will chew on every bite of *God's Chewable Vitamin "C" for the Spirit*.

(trade paper) ISBN 0914984845   **$6.95**

Other Books by Starburst Publishers

(Partial listing— full list available on request)

God's Vitamin "C" for the Spirit of MEN

—D. Larry Miller

Subtitled: *"Tug-at-the-Heart" Stories to Encourage and Strengthen Your Spirit.* Compiled in the format of best-selling *God's Vitamin "C" for the Spirit,* this book is filled with unique and inspiring stories that men of all ages will immediately relate to. True stories by some of the most-loved Christian speakers and writers on topics such as Integrity, Mentoring, Leadership, Marriage, Success/Failure, Family, Godliness, and Spiritual Life are sure to encourage men through the challenges of life. Contributors include Bill McCartney, Tony Evans, Larry Crabb, Tim Kimmel, Billy Graham, and R. C. Sproul, to name a few.

(trade paper) ISBN 0914984810   **$12.95**

God's Chewable Vitamin "C" for the Spirit of DADs

Subtitled: *A Dose of Godly Character, One Bite at a Time.* Scriptures coupled with insightful quotes to inspire men through the changes of life. This little "portable" is the perfect gift for men of all ages and walks of life. It provides the encouragement needed by Dad from time to time.

(trade paper) ISBN 0914984829   **$6.95**

Purchasing Information:

Listed books are available from your favorite Bookstore, either from current stock or special order. To assist bookstores in locating your selection be sure to give title, author, and ISBN #. If unable to purchase from the bookstore you may order direct from STARBURST PUBLISHERS. When ordering, enclose full payment plus $3.00 for shipping and handling ($4.00 if Canada or Overseas). Payment in US Funds only. Please allow two to three weeks minimum (longer overseas) for delivery. Make checks payable to and mail to STARBURST PUBLISHERS, P.O. Box 4123, LANCASTER, PA 17604. Prices subject to change without notice. Catalog available for a 9 x 12 self-addressed envelope with 4 first-class stamps. 9-96